A FUTURE OF CAPITALISM

A Future of Capitalism

The Economic Vision of Robert Heilbroner

Michael C. Carroll
Assistant Professor of Economics
Muskingum College

First published in Great Britain 1998 by
MACMILLAN PRESS LTD
Houndmills, Basingstoke, Hampshire RG21 6XS and London
Companies and representatives throughout the world

A catalogue record for this book is available from the British Library.

ISBN 0–333–67363–8

First published in the United States of America 1998 by
ST. MARTIN'S PRESS, INC.,
Scholarly and Reference Division,
175 Fifth Avenue, New York, N.Y. 10010

ISBN 0–312–17754–2

Library of Congress Cataloging-in-Publication Data
Carroll, Michael C., 1958–
A future of capitalism : the economic vision of Robert L.
Heilbroner / by Michael C. Carroll.
p. cm.
Includes bibliographical references and index.
ISBN 0–312–17754–2 (cloth)
1. Heilbroner, Robert L. 2. Economists—United States.
3. Economics—United States. 4. Capitalism. I. Title.
HB119.H44C37 1997
330.12'2—dc21   97–26473
                                                           CIP

HB
119
.H44
C37
1998
2 an. 1999

© Michael C. Carroll 1998

This book is printed on paper suitable for recycling and made from fully managed and sustained forest sources.

10   9   8   7   6   5   4   3   2   1
07 06 05 04 03 02 01 00 99 98

Printed and bound in Great Britain by
Antony Rowe Ltd, Chippenham, Wiltshire

For my wife
Cyndi

Contents

Preface

Since I began this study almost two years ago, I have had the pleasure of speaking to a large number of fellow economists from around the globe about the substance of Heilbroner's work. At every conference and academic meeting it is interesting to note that the first comment I receive is always some expression of admiration of Heilbroner's writing style; how much each had 'enjoyed' his books. Rarely do they begin by agreeing or disagreeing with the content of his economics.

I hope in some small way this volume can contribute to an appreciation of Heilbroner's work as a whole. There is a serious message in his carefully crafted words. His thirty-plus books and hundreds of articles offer a social analysis unlike that of any modern economist. His approach is holistic, sociopolitical and always penetrating. It clearly deserves to be understood.

While I cannot thank all who have helped me with this work, I must, however, single out the efforts of my brother Mark R. Carroll for his careful reading of the many revisions of this manuscript. His help and inspiration have led to so many improvements of this volume. Any misconceptions or overt mistakes in this work are of course my own and not his.

I would like to acknowledge the efforts of Terrel Gallaway and N. Shilling. They willingly listened to all my rambling and always returned a thoughtful reply. Also, Alice Sherrill, Leota Wolf, Ava Darr, Gerri Ford, and Duane Pool have all contributed in their own way.

I would also like to thank Robert Heilbroner for his inspiration and assistance early in this project. His generosity and openness have made this project possible. Further, I must thank my wife Cyndi for her patience and understanding. I could never have finished without her help.

Finally, I am especially grateful for the generous advice and guidance of J. Ron Stanfield. He has forever opened my eyes to the true world of economics. This, of course, is a debt I can never repay.

Portions of this book are taken from a dissertation submitted to the Academic Faculty of Colorado State University in partial fulfilment of the requirements for a degree of Ph.D.

1 Introduction

The political economy of Robert Heilbroner is something of an enigma in the modern world of 'technical' economics. His writing is not littered with the usual scientific trappings of theorems, lemmas, propositions or paradoxes. Even the most casual inquiry into his work reveals his preference for elegant prose and his indifference to curves and functions. Heilbroner has spent years criticizing the reductionist theory of mainstream economics. He calls modern economic theory irrelevant, a veil, a theology and even the equivalent of 'medieval scholasticism'. In spite of this criticism, he is universally respected by the very people he reproaches. The central body of conservative American economics, The American Economic Association, has even elected him to the influential advisory board for *The Journal of Economic Perspectives*. The profession buys his books by the thousands and lists his work on their syllabi around the world.

Why should a profession so enamoured with mathematical precision be so mesmerized by Heilbroner's classical approach to economics? The answer is clear; he simply asks the right questions. His broad approach allows him the freedom to explore the socioeconomic issues that are out of reach of reductionist theorists. Heilbroner's economics is not hidden behind a wall of scientific jargon. It is not erected on a scaffolding of simplifying assumptions or causal laws. Heilbroner's economics boldly faces the human condition. He clears away the artificial complexities of modern economic life and examines the underlying social fundamentals. He asks direct questions like: 'Is there hope for man?' (Heilbroner 1974a) or 'Is economic theory possible?' (Heilbroner 1966). This is not the research agenda of a traditional economist.

This work provides an intellectual portrait of Robert Heilbroner. It traces the development of Heilbroner's thought and finds that he is a writer of political economy in the classical sense. Reminiscent of Smith or Marx, Heilbroner's economic vision is an unflinching confrontation with the human condition. The depth and breadth of Heilbroner's 'worldly philosophy' cannot be properly appreciated if one approaches looking for an alliance with a single school of thought or with too narrowly defined expectations. Unlike contemporary reductionist theory, Heilbroner's economics is built on a solid foundation of evolutionary dynamics, social psychology and an acute sensitivity to

human history. This holistic orientation affords Heilbroner a wide
degree of methodological freedom to determine both the boundaries
of the object to be studied and the constitutive elements of the discipline that studies it. Heilbroner approaches economics from the perspective of seeing it as a formation of systematized power and of the
resulting socialized beliefs by which that power is depicted as a natural
and necessary form of social life. As the limitations of reductionist
economics become more evident, Heilbroner's *hermeneutic* approach
to economic inquiry grows increasingly important.

This work will show how a comprehensive understanding of the
capitalist social order is paramount to appreciating the full implications of the Heilbroner model. For Heilbroner, capitalism cannot be
adequately conceptualized as an economic system. Whereas most economists naively define capitalism as a *market society* or *free enterprise
system*, Heilbroner believes that it is more properly understood as a
social totality. While it is true that markets and capitalism are inextricably linked, to solely define capitalism in terms of mutual exchange
is to completely miss its essence. Capitalism is not a result of egalitarian metaphysics. Heilbroner believes capitalism is better viewed as a
historical formation that has its own unique nature and logic which
distinguish it from parallel and preceding social formations. Specifically, capitalism is a social order, built upon a deeply embedded core of
internalized values and institutions whose perpetual metamorphosis
appeases regime-like objectives and bestows an overall character that
is typically associated with kingship or predatory war-machines. Personal domination, social superiority, prestige and glory are all
denominated through and by capitalism's internal motion – the insatiable drive for accumulation.

Heilbroner believes the construct of mainstream economics is thor-
oughly ill-equipped to provide any cogent understanding of such a
complex socioeconomic formation. At its best, 'analytical economics',
as Heilbroner refers to conventional theory, can tell us little about the
nature of the social order in which we live. At its worst, it exerts a
systematic distortion over our perception by deliberately deflecting the
emphasis away from capitalism's endemic dynamics and towards an
investigation of superficial price movements. In reality, a market price
is simply a conveniently visible epiphenomenon which bobs innocently
on the surface of modern business society. By its very nature, mainstream economics lacks the penetrating vision required to describe
capitalism; conventional economic science simply asks the wrong questions. To understand capitalism, what is required is an approach to

economics that is not constrained by the limited description of economic reality, but instead searches for an order and meaning in man's social history on a much grander scale. In short, what is required is the worldly philosophy of Robert Heilbroner.

This book highlights how Robert Heilbroner's economic model is actually a comprehensive critique of social interaction. It places Heilbroner within intellectual history, and examines the significance of Heilbroner's unique contribution to the development of past and future economic thought and policy formation. Furthermore, it addresses the myth that Heilbroner is merely a master wordsmith and that his writings are simply a distillation of complex economic issues into a form palatable to a general audience. Nothing could be further from the truth. Heilbroner's work provides a very inclusive socioeconomic model and this book will emphasize the holistic nature of his contribution to the understanding of capitalism.

STRUCTURE OF THE WORK

The following chapter 'The Man and His Vision' (Chapter 2) examines the life of Robert Heilbroner. It traces the development of his thought and 'radical–conservative' ideology. Further, it details the significant influence of men like Paul Sweezy, Joseph Schumpeter, and most of all, Adolph Lowe. It traces his major works and places them into historical context.

'Limitations of Traditional Economics' (Chapter 3) explores Heilbroner's critique of current economic theory. It shows that he believes that modern economic science simply asks the wrong questions. He believes that scarcity-based allocation theory may address only the surface of the capitalist order. Further, the hypothetico-deductive methodology of neoclassical theory rests on a core of behavioural assumptions that may no longer be valid in a modern capitalist society. The chapter explores Heilbroner's belief that modern theory acts as a veil which actually obscures the true economic problem.

Chapter 4 'The Methodology of Worldly Philosophy' presents Heilbroner's *hermeneutic* methodology. The chapter opens with an examination of his 'worldly philosophers'. It finds that Heilbroner draws extensively from their sociopolitical orientation and wide-ranging vision. Next, the chapter details the specifics of Heilbroner's socioeconomic model. The model can be described as a triad of understandings. The core is composed of a thorough understanding of the human condition. Once the basic behavioural properties are in place, Heilbroner proceeds to a sociopolitical analysis. He examines the cultural and institutional aspects of human interaction. Heilbroner ultimately rests his economic theory upon this sociohistorical foundation.

'The Structure of Capitalism' (Chapter 5) is an intense look at Heilbroner's definition of the capitalist structure. It shows why Heilbroner views capitalism as a 'regime' and how it evolved as a distinct historical formation. It explores the three defining characteristics of capitalism – the drive to accumulate, the existence of markets and the division of power into public and private realms.

Chapter 6 'A View to the Future' examines Heilbroner's reputation as a social prognosticator. It details his approach to economic prediction and finds that it relies on the historical logic contained in the unfolding of the capitalist order. He believes that capitalism will be the dominant social order in the twenty-first century but the internal dynamics of the capitalist accumulation make it unlikely that the system can last forever.

The last chapter 'A Final Appraisal' (Chapter 7) sums up Heilbroner's extensive contribution to economic thought. It provides a summary of this work and examines his changing views on the future of the capitalist order. It also attempts to properly place his work within some accepted school of thought. It finds that while the label Marxist, Institutionalist or Radical explains portions of his writing, only the term 'Worldly Philosopher' comes close to defining the essence of the work.

2 The Man and His Vision

Robert Heilbroner is one of the most widely read economists of the twentieth century. His rare ability to distill complex economic jargon into clear elegant prose has allowed his numerous books and articles to enjoy considerable popularity with the general public as well as the academic community. Generations of economists have cut their teeth on his 1953 classic, *The Worldly Philosophers*, currently in its sixth edition with well over three million copies in print. This book, or 'annuity' in Heilbroner's words, has lured more than one unsuspecting soul into the dark world of economics. The success of this text in recruiting today's practising economists has even led some to say that Heilbroner is responsible, to some small degree, for the state of economic science today. I am sure that such high praise from his peers would make Heilbroner very, very uncomfortable. Sidestepping for the moment the obvious trepidations of bearing accountability for the 'dismal science', to say Heilbroner is responsible for the state of modern economics is quite a stretch. For that matter, to call Heilbroner an economist is also a stretch. Heilbroner often shirks the label economist in favour of 'intellectual', 'economic historian' or 'economic sociologist'. He has never concerned himself with the typical model building and mathematical statements that are the cornerstone of modern-day reductionist theory. In fact, he has gone so far as to say:

> I'm certainly not interested in spinning out theology like the model builders. Economists are enamored with model building which I see as an attempt of extraordinary hubris to reduce the economic world to mathematical statements. I'm skeptical about technological coefficients and behavioral equations. If all economic theory disappeared, the acuity of economic policy would not be affected one iota. (Heilbroner 1972, 59)

Are these the words of a typical, twentieth-century, card-carrying economist? The answer has to be no. However, are these the words of a man frustrated by the narrowing focus of reductionist economics; a man who sees economics in a more classical light, looking for order and meaning on a much grander scale? That answer has to be yes. So while the majority of the discipline tinker with stylized axioms and statistical methods, Heilbroner simply tries to 'bring an economic point of view to social and political problems' (Heilbroner 1972, 59) and not get entangled in the minutiae of economics. He works within the scale of the political economist of the eighteenth or nineteenth century. He roots his economics firmly within the stream of human history, constantly seeking the essence of economic activity; the very nature and logic of man's provisioning systems. His economic scenarios are much more encompassing than anything which could be called macroeconomic models. In short, Robert Heilbroner is working with a vision of economics that is most sympathetic to what he has called the 'worldly philosophy'.

Heilbroner's vision, his 'worldly' approach to economics, is so completely different from the mainstream economics that we must spend time defining the influences which shaped his outlook. For this reason, I think it would be impossible to understand Heilbroner's work without first exploring the man himself, his life, background and academic influences. It is important that we remember that the only true common denominator to a lifetime's work is the man himself.

I use this opening chapter to provide a brief biographical sketch of Heilbroner's life. I will attempt to convey enough of a personal portrait so that the reader gets some sense of who the man is, who his major influences were, and which personal qualities reflect through into his work. While this is clearly not intended to be a psychological profile, I do believe it is imperative that we get a sense of the man before we move on to his work proper.

THE LIFE OF ROBERT HEILBRONER

Robert Louis Heilbroner was born on the upper West Side of Manhattan on 24 March 1919, the third child and only son of Louis and Helen (Weiller) Heilbroner. His father Louis was the cofounder of Weber & Heilbroner Inc., a chain of men's clothing stores. The family's business success enabled Robert and his sisters to attend private schools and to generally 'grow up like anyone else in the privileged class.'[1] Growing up in this exclusive environment, it would be usual to expect the development of fairly conservative and predictable political views. This was not to be in Heilbroner's case. One-dimensional definitions such as *liberal, radical* or *conservative* cannot sufficiently capture his scope of social thinking. Heilbroner actually classes himself as a 'radical–conservative'.[2] He has taken elements from each ideology and blended them into his own social outlook. He explains:

I'm radical in that I see capitalism in its historical context, in the process of flux, and I support many changes toward equality that are called 'socialism'... But I'm conservative in that I no longer believe institutional change will make the problems go away. There are questions that conservatives bring to the fore that are ignored by radicals and liberals: the human condition, man's capacity for evil. The radicals do not ask these large questions. (Heilbroner 1972, 59)

This very different ideological classification has clearly influenced his economics. It sets the stage for large-scale economic inquiry that does not fall neatly within any traditional doctrine. Within Heilbroner's work one can see elements from people like Karl Marx, Adam Smith and Thomas Malthus. While each of these men are traditionally championed as icons of their own very different ideologies, they each share a common footing in Heilbroner's economics. Heilbroner is no slave to a single social dogma. He actually states that it is evident from his writings that 'liberal, radical and conservative promptings have successively colored my social philosophy' (Heilbroner 1992a, 247).

The combination of two early childhood events may help us account for the development of his social views. The first was the death of his father Louis when Robert was only five and the second was the Great Depression.

Louis Heilbroner died in 1925 at the age of 45. It was less the shock of his father's death that influenced Heilbroner than the resulting closeness with what he calls his 'substitute father', the family chauffeur. He credits this man with instilling in him his lifelong egalitarian and 'radical–conservative' tendencies. An interesting and previously quoted (see Okroi 1988) passage from a 1975 *Psychology Today* interview best displays this personal transformation:

My family was middle-class and conventional, so I grew up in an environment that would normally have made me conservative. But then something happened. My father died when I was about five years old. And from then on, for about ten years I found myself with another father, so to speak. He was the family chauffeur, and he was a fine, warm-hearted man. I loved him very much. But at the same time he was an employee. And although my mother was a good person, this man I loved so much was essentially a servant to her. Moreover, he didn't like being a servant. He hated his uniform, called it his monkey suit. I was acutely conscious of the fact that he had been thrust into a position of inferiority by economic circumstances, and I deeply felt his humiliation. I've thought about this story for quite a while now, and I think it explains something about my life and personality and hence about my work. I've found myself pulled between conservative standards on the one hand, and a strong feeling for the underdog on the other. (Campbell 1975, 98)

Heilbroner firmly believes this awakening of his egalitarian tendencies significantly changed the 'temper and substance' of his books. After writing *The Worldly Philosophers* in 1953 the wish to break through social facades became even stronger. His own 'worldly philosophy' was beginning to edge to the fore. However, none of this explains why he turned to economics as his primary vehicle. For that we must look to another dramatic event, namely the Great Depression:

I was aware of a presence called the Depression. I remember an enormous headline in late October of 1929 in the evening newspaper *The Sun*, but at age ten I had no idea what the word 'crash' meant. I found out in school, where the joke went around that hotel clerks were supposed to ask 'For sleeping or jumping?' when someone inquired about rooms. That winter two fathers of school friends jumped.   (Heilbroner 1993b, 100)

Harvard

While not directly affected by unemployment or devastating poverty, Heilbroner was significantly influenced by the Depression. Even though he viewed the Depression somewhat at arms length, he still found it very 'oppressive and incomprehensible' (Heilbroner 1993b, 100). This blend of unease and curiosity helped push Heilbroner into economics when he entered Harvard. Although he originally planned a degree in English, he states that: 'When I went to Harvard in 1936, I took economics[3] because I thought it would help me understand the nature of that mysterious presence [the Great Depression]' (Heilbroner 1993b, 101). He found that the Depression was as much of a mystery for the professors as it was to him. In the late 1930s the economics profession had no significant explanation of this catastrophic event. Maturing corporate capitalism had never experienced such a catastrophic meltdown. Classical economic theory predicted that the economy would soon adjust and the country would return to normal. It did not. The Depression lingered and economists had no explanation. We must remember that economics was a very young 'science'. The scientific '*ics*' – like physics and mathematics – had only recently been added to the word economy. Heilbroner writes: 'It is difficult today to convey the sense of discovery that permeated economics in the late 1930s, when neither growth nor general equilibrium, rational expectations, or any kind of expectations, choice theoretics or, for that matter, micro nor macro had yet entered the vocabulary' (Heilbroner 1992a, 241). Heilbroner turned to economics looking for answers at the very time the profession was undergoing a most difficult revolution: the Keynesian revolution.

In the late 1930s Harvard was a place of heated debates and stubborn opinions. Heilbroner recalls:

> One of my most vivid academic recollections was a debate mounted by the economics faculty in a crowded hall, where distinguished professors argued with trembling voices and empurpled faces as to whether savings did or did not equal investment.
>
> (Heilbroner 1992a, 241)

Heilbroner had entered Harvard the very year Keynes published his classic, *The General Theory of Employment, Interest and Money*. The ideas Keynes presented were radically different from the standard theories. Keynes's emphasis on fiscal rather than monetary policy was a radically foreign concept.

The Keynesian revolution did not come easily to most American universities. Harvard, however, had an edge; an edge named Alvin Hansen. Hansen was Keynes's foremost American disciple. In his seminar on Fiscal Policy, Hansen exerted a profound influence on a generation of graduate students and fellow faculty. Co-taught with John E. Williams (Blaug 1985) the seminar espoused Keynesian ideas and fiscal economics. It was certainly a hotbed of debate. Heilbroner recalls Joseph Schumpeter lecturing in Hansen's course that 'a depression is for capitalism a good cold douche' (Heilbroner 1992a, 241). This statement was all the more shocking before they realized that for Schumpeter, a *douche* was a shower.

Heilbroner's first economic publication was a Keynesian paper in the *American Economic Review* (1942) entitled 'Saving and Investment: Dynamic Aspects'. However, in our study of Heilbroner, I do not believe the content of Keynesian economics is as important as the environment it created at Harvard. It is difficult to imagine the energy which must have existed. The combination of professors like Alvin Hansen, John Williams, J. K. Galbraith, Paul Sweezy, Wassily

Leontief and Edward Mason with students like Heilbroner, Samuelson and Tobin must have been a very volatile mix.

Heilbroner graduated Harvard *summa cum laude* and Phi Beta Kappa in 1940, majoring in history, government and economics. After graduation he worked for a brief time at the Office of Price Administration. He was drafted into the army after learning Japanese at military intelligence school, and spent the war in the Pacific as an interpreter of Japanese. He earned a bronze star for his army service.

Returning from the war in 1946, Heilbroner went to work as an economist for a company that specialized in international trade and commodities. At the same time he was driven by his desire to write and his interest in economics. He began taking his writing to the office rather than his work home. *Harper's* magazine picked up an article and he decided he would rather write than 'trade tea' (Van Dyne 1978) and quit the trading house. The article 'The American Poor' (Heilbroner 1950) eventually made the cover of *Harper's* and Heilbroner left the trading company and never went back to the private sector.

Adolph Lowe and The New School

At the same time he made arguably his most significant professional decision and enrolled in the graduate programme at the New School for Social Research. There he would meet a man whose influence would shape his life forever. In the autumn of 1946 Robert Heilbroner met Adolph Lowe. Heilbroner recalls:

> On the first day of class, fifteen or twenty students, some like myself in their mid twenties, others considerably older, looked with varying degrees of nervousness or composure on our instructor, who looked back at us with equal curiosity... The appointed hour having struck, he began to talk, and I was acutely conscious that my graduate education had commenced. In my earlier schooling at Harvard I had heard many famous lecturers, but never anyone like Adolph Lowe... It was magic. Better, it was the very embodiment of teaching, for the virtuoso exposition, which evoked feelings of respect verging on awe, never prevented – indeed, seemed to encourage – the most timid student from raising a hand when there was something to be further explained, or a point to be made, or an objection lodged.
>
> (Heilbroner 1990, ix)

Lowe would become his most ardent supporter and most severe critic. The bond that developed between Heilbroner and Lowe is something unique in academic circles. For nearly half a century, Lowe successively played the role of mentor, advisor, critic, colleague and confidant. After Lowe retired from the New School (1975) and had moved back to Germany[4] (1982), the two remained close. They corresponded regularly with 'letters of praise and criticism mixed in with personal and school gossip, philosophical and technical problems with family news and occasional soul searching' (Heilbroner 1990, xii). Their deep friendship would last until Lowe's passing in the summer of 1995 at the age of 102.

Adolph Lowe was far and away the most influential character in Heilbroner's economic development. Heilbroner's approach to economics – as a social inquirer and not a technical model builder – clearly mirrors Lowe. Like Heilbroner, Lowe worked on the more radical fringes of the economics profession. When Lowe won the Veblen– Commons Award in 1979, he wrote to his friend Sir Geoffrey Vickers, saying that he had won the 'bad boy' award. He explained that the 'Clark Medal was for the "good boys" who accept the ruling neoclassical framework and the Veblen prize was for the "bad boys" who doubt the fruitfulness of orthodoxy and work on different lines' (Vickers 1990, 168). When Heilbroner accepted his own Veblen–Commons Award in 1994, he spoke of Lowe's influence:

> Adolph Lowe was crucial to my economic education in two ways. One was that he was deeply skeptical of the tautologies and formalisms that already exist in his day were coming more and more to displace the historical and institutional approach that he believed to be essential for economic understanding... He made me a policy-minded interventionist... The other reason that Lowe played so significant a part in my development was that he led me into the field that has become my speciality. It was in his seminars on Smith, Ricardo, and Marx that I began to see economics as a succession of extraordinary social dramas – a perception that led me to write *The Worldly Philosophers* while I was still a student.   (Heilbroner 1994, 325–6)

It is interesting to note that Adolph Lowe was not enthusiastic about his student undertaking *The Worldly Philosophers* project. At first he declared 'that you cannot do!'[5] Later, after Heilbroner had written three chapters and submitted them to Lowe for comment, Lowe returned and said 'That you must do!'

The Worldly Philosophers

The release of *The Worldly Philosophers* marks the beginning for Heilbroner's economic influence. While he had published economic articles before, *The Worldly Philosophers* in 1953 would set the stage for his long-term success. The book drew rave reviews in academia as well as in the popular press which has pushed the book into its sixth edition and multiplied the initial printing a thousand-fold. At the time of its introduction, Heilbroner was unaware that Edward Gibbon had already used the term 'worldly philosopher' in his classic *The Decline and Fall of the Roman Empire*. In fact Heilbroner had originally toyed with calling the book *The Money Philosophers*. He was not quite happy with the title and subsequently discussed it over lunch with the then editor of *Harper's*, Frederick Lewis Allen. Heilbroner said he knew 'money' wasn't right and Allen said 'you mean *'worldly'*. Heilbroner bought the lunch.

The Worldly Philosophers is the first glimpse we get into Heilbroner's treatment of economic history as a 'succession of social dramas'. He sees *economics* as a way to investigate the whole of social provisioning. I will spend much more time on this in Chapter 3, but for now we need to appreciate just how different this is from traditional economic theory. He is swimming against the neoclassical drift into reductionist theory. At the time when the profession was closing in on itself with mathematical postulates and stringent statistical modelling, Heilbroner was widening his work to include elements of human behaviour and sociopolitical disruptions. His study of economic life did not fit into the *science* of economics. He knew his work did not fit into the new mould. He once said in a *Business Week* interview: 'I think I'm regarded ambivalently by the profession: as useful but not quite legitimate' (Heilbroner 1972, 59).

His second book, *The Quest For Wealth: A Study of Acquisitive Man* (1956), continued his move away from mainstream economics. In *Quest for Wealth* we get a glimpse of the more psychological grounding his work would take. He explores the psychological roots of man's acquisitive nature. Looking back we can see that this book was his first attempt at exploring the 'human nature' which lies beneath all the institutions that exist in any social system. This look at the human underpinnings of any society did not really mature until his third book, *The Future As History: The Historic Currents of Our Time and the Direction in Which They are Taking America* (1959). The central tenet of this book is that economic development was a revolutionary and not an evolutionary process. *The Future as History* was written against the backdrop of the general optimism of the late 1950s. In the book, Heilbroner argues that economic development is more likely to occur in a 'strong man' or military regime rather than be the consequence of free-market interactions. This distanced Heilbroner even more from the economic mainstream. However, it did establish him as a well-respected 'Social Critic'. The book was very well received and had a significant impact.

For most of his contemporaries, this idea of revolutionary economic development placed Heilbroner firmly in the 'radical' camp. Anything that smacked of revolution was quickly dubbed radical. However, there is a definite conservative theme to the book. In the latter parts of the book he asks larger more typically 'conservative' questions. The subtitles of the closing chapter include 'The Limits of the Possible', 'The Inertia of History' and 'The Ambiguity of Events'. Heilbroner would say: 'These subtitles indicate a facet of my inquiries that has distanced me from conventional views of the left as well as the right. The distancing arises from a recognition of the power of social resistance to change' (Heilbroner 1992a, 244).

Ph.D.

Heilbroner entered the early 1960s with a growing list of very successful publications but without a Ph.D. Not wanting to disrupt the conversational tone (and market appeal) of *The Worldly Philosophers* he did not sufficiently document the text enough to be considered a scholarly dissertation. Over the next several years he continued to write books and articles but never produced a dissertation. He never gave up the idea of a Ph.D. and in fact did start several other dissertation projects. One was a study of Ricardian economics which he abandoned after six months because he said it looked like a five-year project. He also got involved in a Nelson Rockefeller–Henry Kissinger commission which he eventually resigned and called it 'the most egregious misuse of research studies to serve predetermined conclusions' (Van Dyne 1978). He also conducted a study of stock ownership which he later abandoned when someone at another university published a very similar study. He had just started yet another project, a study of the service sector, when he got an invitation to teach at Berkeley without his Ph.D. While spending the summer on Martha's Vineyard, he wrote to Lowe saying that he did not have the heart to complete the 'service sector study' and explained the offer he had received from

Berkeley. Heilbroner said 'I had this long list of well-known economists who didn't have their Ph.D.'s so I said the hell with it' (Van Dyne 1978). He ended up not accepting the Berkeley offer and returned to the New School. However, the spectre of the dissertation did not disappear. He tells a story of seeing the president of the New School:

> One day I passed the president in the hall, and he said, 'Well, Bob how goes the dissertation?' I told him I'd dropped the whole idea and didn't want the damned Ph.D. He gave me a curious look, because he was on his way to a faculty meeting where one of the items on the agenda was a proposal to grant me a Ph.D. using as my dissertation a book I had already published called *The Making of Economic Society*.
> (Van Dyne 1978)

Finally in 1963, seventeen years after he had begun his graduate studies, his Ph.D. was awarded and he joined the Graduate Faculty of the New School For Social Research. He even delivered the vale-dictory address at his belated commencement.

A Primer on Government Spending

1963 also marked the release of his book *A Primer on Government Spending* which he co-authored with Peter Bernstein. The book addressed government spending at a time when fiscal policy was new and still misunderstood. This confusion over government spending has not disappeared. The book's opening lines could easily have been written today and not some thirty-odd years past:

> This book springs from the belief that many people are worried about government spending ... It is understandable that government spending should conjure up these worries, for it deals with a lexicon of worrisome terms – debts and deficits – and talks in a language of profligacy – tens of hundreds of billions of dollars.
> (Heilbroner and Bernstein 1963, 11)

The book represents a major theme in Heilbroner's work: the role of government in the economic process. It also is one of the few areas of 'economic policy' on which Heilbroner has taken a stand. He tends to shy away from economic policy because it assumes the underpinning political process and economic theory is all right. As the next chapter indicates, Heilbroner would never agree to that. The limited research agenda of the neoclassical model makes any policy recommendation a very dangerous commodity.

A Primer on Government Spending was a success and Heilbroner and Bernstein followed with a sequel in 1989 with *The Debt and Deficit: False Alarms, Real Possibilities*. The *Primer* was widely read outside of academic circles and is reported to have had significant influence on the policy makers of the day. In the preface of the second book, Heilbroner and Bernstein tell a story of how President John F. Kennedy had read the manuscript and actually found a spelling error.

The proper role for government is closely associated with the ideological questions of socialism and capitalism. The large-scale pressures of capitalism versus socialism become the centre of his work. Throughout the 1960s and early 1970s, Heilbroner would write on the social institutions. In books like *The Great Ascent* (1963), *The Limits of American Capitalism* (1965), and *Between Capitalism and Socialism* (1970), Heilbroner explores American hegemony in economic development and economic activity in changing social environments. All of this work was considered 'radical'. In fact the 1960s would be his transition from 'liberal' to more 'radical'. As I said earlier in this chapter, he admits that over his career he has moved from liberal to radical to more conservative in his ideological colouring. In the middle 1960s the New School took on a more radical orientation. As people like E. J. Nell, Stephen Hymer, Anwar Shaikh and David Gordon joined the faculty, more 'radical' publications began to flow from the New School. It was at this time that Heilbroner began his more detailed study of Marx. At the time of *The Worldly Philosophers*, Heilbroner had only studied the *Manifesto*, Volume I of *Capital*, and *Theories of Surplus Value*. His more comprehensive study of Marx would have to wait until after he became Chair of Economics at the New School in 1968 and the Norman Thomas Chair in 1972.

Marxism: For and Against

His Marxist studies would culminate in his 1980 book *Marxism: For and Against*. Although he wrote a number of very influential volumes in the 1970s – and I will soon return to these – I believe it is important to continue to mine the 'radical' vein to its logical conclusion. *Marxism: For and Against* evoked praise, condemnation and bewilderment from its readers. For many, the book is one of the most accessible explanations of Marxist thought and it has found its way onto a large number of syllabi and is particularly useful in undergraduate courses as the student's first view of the often impenetrable Marx.

It was, however, not without its criticisms and outright bewilderment. Some thought the work was an 'apologia' for Marxism.[6] It was not the 'For' or the 'Against' that drew most of the criticism; it was the 'and'. Many had no idea how someone could be *for* and *against* Marxism. Marxist thought has always carried an enormous amount of emotional baggage, and the idea that someone could be divided, and yet unified, on the issue was for many nothing short of blasphemy. For Heilbroner, it is actually the 'and' which most accurately expresses his scholarship. The best reconciliation of this duality comes in his own words and provides one of the best short explanations of his social theory. In 1992 he explains:

> In fact, the conjunction 'and' describes very precisely my intellectual stance. In the book I define Marxism as consisting of four inter-related but distinct parts: (i) a dialectical approach to knowledge, construed as a relational rather than a positivist epistemology; (ii) a materialist conception of history, centering on the importance of production activities, and class struggle over distribution; (iii) a general view of capitalism that emphasized the ideological aspects of Marxian economics – above all, its demystification of 'labor' and 'capital' as comprised of social relations, not individuals or things; and (iv) the commitment to socialism, defined as the practice of Marxian social theory. This four-way definition allowed me to see Marxism 'as embodying the promise of a grand synthesis of human understanding – a synthesis that begins with a basic philosophic perspective, goes on to apply this perspective to the interpretation of history, moves thereafter to an analysis of the present as the working-out of historical forces in the existing social order, and culminates in an orientation to the future that continues the line of analysis in an unbroken trajectory of action.' At the same time, the categorization of Marxism also allowed me to define my stance *for* the first three elements mentioned above, and *against* the last – namely, a commitment to socialism as an historical destination which can be attained by 'scientifically' guided analysis.

(Heilbroner 1992a, 223–4)

Along the radical-to-conservative continuum, this explanation would certainly place Heilbroner at the more radical end of the spectrum. He writes of class struggles over distribution, a materialist view of history, and demystification. In our look at Heilbroner's life and work, it would be convenient to pigeonhole him as a Marxist or at least a radical. This classification would clearly capture the essence of much of his economics and he has often been labelled a socialist or democratic socialist in the press. The problem is, there is more to the man than meets the eye at any time. We must evoke his 'For' and 'Against' any ideological label we apply to him. That is why his own label of 'radical–conservative' is actually a very accurate representation. While *Marxism: For and Against* overtly examined the radical Marxist model, it covertly raised questions of a more conservative nature. It expanded his inquiry into the human responsiveness to social change that was first introduced in *The Future as History*. It asked if the human species contained any fundamental compatibility with a social order like socialism.

During his comprehensive study of Marx in the 1970s, he wrote a number of books which were not openly 'Marxist'.[7] *An Inquiry Into the Human Prospect* (1974) examines the ecological issues that were beginning to draw considerable attention. The book examines ecological problems like global warming and increases in population growth. It is often touted as a very dark and pessimistic view of the world's ecological problems. The book, however, is less about the gloom and doom of the pending environmental crisis than it is about latent human responsiveness. He opens the book with the question: 'Is there hope for man?' (Heilbroner 1974a, 11). He is not questioning the overt environmental damages but rather the fundamental human ability to respond to massive external threats. In particular he was questioning capitalism or socialism's ability to orchestrate suitable control measures to deal with problems of this magnitude. The latter chapters of this book will present Heilbroner's answers to these questions. Chapter 4 specifically looks at his view of capitalism and Chapter 5 will look at his view of the future.

Capitalism and Socialism

Returning to our mostly chronological look at Heilbroner life, we see that in the 1980s he directed his focus to the study of the socio-economic systems of capitalism and socialism. In 1985 he published *The Nature and Logic of Capitalism*. This book directly examines the general behaviour-shaping institutions which endow any social order with its own distinct 'nature', and the 'logic' which impels the system with its historic dynamic. This, of course, is a very different didactic approach from simply treating capitalism as a market system or socialism as a command system. Heilbroner is again looking below the patina of the social order. This continues to distance him from conventional economists. What he is actually doing is moving from the 'positivist' methods of the economic science and moving toward a more *hermeneutic*[8] approach to economic inquiry. This can also be interpreted as a return to his attempts to discover the deeper roots of 'worldly philosophy'. *The Nature and Logic of Capitalism* and his entry 'Capitalism' in *The New Palgrave* (1986) are two of the best investigations of the capitalist order. They see capitalism as a historical epoch, or regime. Similar to kingship or primitive orders, capitalism is a collection of institutional constraints which is motivated by a central behavioural tendency. In other societies, this central motivation may have been military domination or tribal prestige. In capitalism the motivation is the drive to accumulate capital.

The late 1980s marks a very significant turn in Heilbroner's work. He begins to see that socialism may not be a plausible social structure. He directly addresses this in a 1989 article in *The New Yorker* (Heilbroner 1989). Later in the same year, in an interview with *New Perspective Quarterly*, he states:

> For the first time this century – and for the first time in my life – I would argue that socialism has no plausible economic framework. Only half a century ago, the great question was how rapidly the transformation from capitalism to socialism would take place...
> Now, the great question of the last years of this century must be posed the other way: Will socialism evolve into some form of capitalism.   (Sheinbaum and Gardels 1989, 4)

This reversal of views was not solely brought about by the decline of the Soviet Union. Heilbroner had been writing about this for many years. Articles like 'Capitalism as Gestalt: A Contrast of Visions' (Heilbroner 1984), 'The Coming Meltdown of Traditional Capitalism'(Heilbroner 1988d), 'The State and Capitalism' (Heilbroner 1985b) set the stage for this change.

This change in the prospects for capitalism should not be misconstrued as a ringing endorsement of the capitalist system. Heilbroner is not singing capitalism's praises. He states:

> Although I am much more sanguine about the economic prospects for capitalism, I am not so sanguine about its civilizational pro-

spects. Capitalism does wonders for economic growth, but little for moral growth or cultural enrichment. Capitalism is full of self-debasement. Witness the commercial vulgarity that pervades our media-hypnotized culture; it is offensive to the human spirit.

(Sheinbaum and Gardels 1989, 7)

Heilbroner's pessimism of capitalist life is reflected in his prognosis for modern economic analysis. In 1988 he published *Behind the Veil of Economics: Essays in the Worldly Philosophy*. This book is a collection of essays which show how economic science becomes a 'veil' which obscures true social understanding. He advocates the idea of viewing economics as a belief system; a system to which the investigator (the economist) is inextricably linked. Any inquiry that the economist may generate is coloured by his association with the system under consideration. This system–investigator linkage is the concept that Schumpeter introduced in 1954. Schumpeter termed it a question of vision. Vision or 'pre-analytic cognitive act' to use Schumpeter's words, directs the initial focus of inquiry – it influences the original interests and questions of the researcher. In *Behind the Veil*, Heilbroner deeply looks at the method of analysis which modern economics employs and finds it lacking. It no longer seeks to explain social provisioning, and is increasingly focused on technical details.

Views to the Future

1989 saw the retirement of Heilbroner from the New School faculty. His *emeritus* status has in no way deterred his flow of publications. In 1993 he published *21st Century Capitalism*; 1995 *Visions of the Future*; and 1996 *The Crisis of Vision in Modern Economic Thought* and *Teachings From the Worldly Philosophy*. All of these books continue to expand and espouse his economic vision. *21st Century Capitalism* and *Visions of the Future* continue his look into the capitalist social order. *Visions* actually provides a good model of his economic method. It also directly leads to his critique of neoclassical theory which he summarizes in *The Crisis of Vision in Modern Economic Thought*. *Crisis*, co-authored with William Milberg looks at a lack of any overarching paradigm in economics since the Keynesian revolution. All of these works clearly demarcate Heilbroner from the rest of the economics profession. He has never aligned himself with any 'school' of thought. While his work complements many, especially American Institutionalism, he has never offered a clear endorsement.

Heilbroner's list of publications continues unabated. It is my hope that this volume may help to put some of his work into perspective. It has been said that Heilbroner is a writer of Galbraithian proportions. This association implies that the work is in some way inferior to Galbraith's. I hope this volume displaces any such inference. In this very brief look at his life and work I have limited the inquiry to but a very select number of his published works. I urge the reader to view the listing of Heilbroner's economic writings to develop a more accurate appreciation of his output. I also remind the reader that even this is in some cases a partial listing of his 'economic' writings. He has published a long list of non-academic and non-economic which I have not included.

At this point I hope we have gained sufficient insight into the man to more rigorously examine his work. We have explored the origins and evolution of his ideology; examined his desire to find the deeper meanings and origins of 'worldly philosophy'; and saw how his extensive mid-career examination of Marx coloured his succeeding work.

In the following chapters we will delve more deeply into the body of his work. We begin with a look at what distances Heilbroner from mainstream economics by looking at his criticism of the neoclassical model. From there we can detail his own economic model and explore his vision of capitalism which is the base of all of his economics.

3 Limitations of Traditional Economics

As stated in the previous chapter, Robert Heilbroner is a writer of political economy of classical dimensions. The breadth of vision that is evident in his range of writings also transfers to the scope of his criticisms of traditional economic theory. Nothing in his work can be properly appreciated unless one understands that his aim is not a simple reconstruction or adaptation of neoclassical economic theory or method; his dissent runs much deeper. He states that over the years he has developed 'an increasing impatience with, and finally a near total rejection of, neoclassical economics as an interpretation of social reality' (Heilbroner 1992a, 247). To Heilbroner, traditional economists simply ask the wrong questions. Such a wide separation makes interpreting the finer points of his contributions difficult. In most critical discussion, both participants share some common footing. The discourse usually begins from this common point and proceeds using a mutually agreed upon vocabulary with each participant attempting to draw the other towards their side of the question. In this case any common ground, including vocabulary, is frequently quite scarce. Heilbroner and the neoclassical school are often so far apart they cannot even agree upon the appropriate goal of the discussion. In other words, what is at stake is the actual definition, scope and correct role of economic science itself.

This chapter highlights the critical points of conflict between the approaches employed by Heilbroner and traditional economic science. I begin with their fundamental differences in the definition of economic inquiry. From there I will proceed with a point by point look at the neoclassical method, highlighting as I go, the key criticisms Heilbroner makes of this traditional method. The chapter concludes with a look at the more subtle and ambiguous differences in Heilbroner's vision, ideology and morality.

DEFINITION OF ECONOMICS

Pick up any traditional economic textbook and you will learn that the science of economics is the study of how society allocates scarce resources in the face of unlimited wants. Neoclassical theorists place scarcity at the root of the economic problem. Furthermore, they increasingly limit themselves by stating that scarcity is a necessary but not sufficient condition. For something to have economic significance it must also be exchangeable. Lord Robbins states in his 1932 classic *An Essay on The Nature and Significance of Economic Science* that:

> The Manna which fell from heaven may have been scarce, but if it was impossible to exchange it for something else or to postpone its use, it was not the object of any activity with an economic aspect.
> (Robbins [1935] 1949, 13)

In other words, society must *economize*[1] its scarce resources through the exchange mechanism of the market with the accompanying limitations of such restraints as relative prices, income and time.

Heilbroner, on the other hand, does not rest his economics on the scant platform of scarcity. Why should scarcity be society's original sin when modern anthropologists tell us that *satiety*, punctuated by periods of acute suffering, and not *scarcity* appears to be the predominant material condition of primitive societies (Sahlins 1972). If economic theory is to have any lasting relevance, then it must survive more than a single historical period. Economics must be more than a theory of market choices. A market theory is of little use explaining the historical epochs when social relations of exchange were determined by tradition or tribal hierarchy. For Heilbroner, the study of economics should 'enable us to better comprehend the structure and tendencies of the economic order – that is, the institutions and activities that affect the production and distribution of wealth' (Heilbroner 1970b, 81). Economics must confront more elemental human patterns than simple material wants and maximizing behaviour. To be useful, it must probe human emotional drives such as social superiority, prestige and glory. Economics must explain the existence and execution of these elementary human instincts within a wide array of historical social configurations, from primitive war-machines to modern corporate capitalism. For Heilbroner, these issues cannot be addressed through the neoclassical methods of abstracting human behaviour and examining market choices. The key lies in a systematic inquiry into the social nature of how wealth and power (individual and the state) are utilized, and denominated, in the various stages of history. Stages which may include a variety of social organizations including tribal hierarchy or the various renditions of capitalism. In short, economics must be approached as 'a form of systematized power and of the socialized beliefs by which that power is depicted as a natural and necessary form of social life' (Heilbroner 1992a, 247).

What sets this form of inquiry apart from that of the traditional economist is Heilbroner's decision to place his method firmly within historical time, and most importantly, place it centrally in a social setting. Heilbroner points out (Heilbroner 1987, 113) that even if one takes the traditional choice theoretic view of economics, one must admit that choices and trade-offs are made *in* society and not *by* society. This is a very critical distinction in understanding Heilbroner's method. His criticisms are not randomly aimed at the obvious simplifications and abstractions of the neoclassical model. His criticisms are directed at strategic deficiencies in the infrastructure of the neoclassical method. Therefore, before we proceed further I must more fully define the methodologies and mythologies of the neoclassical model.

ECONOMICS AS SCIENCE

In his 1968 essay 'Putting Marx to Work',[2] Heilbroner used a quote from the minor nineteenth-century pamphleteer and *philosophe*, Abbé Mably, to set the stage for his fundamental dissent from traditional economic science. Mably asks the innocent question: 'Is society a branch of physics?' This little quote peaks in its absurdity when we realize that the only truthful answer a neoclassical economist can muster is yes. The neoclassical theorist's approach unquestionably is a classic case of physics envy.

The neoclassical economist takes great pride in the fact that his discipline is the most 'scientific' of the social sciences. The level of formal logic, mathematics and statistical inference cannot be matched by any of economics' social science neighbours. The increased prestige for economic science, from the placement of the important 'ics' into its name, to the establishment of a Nobel Prize has been accomplished by increasing the rigour and scientific character of economics.

Neoclassical economists have emulated physical science's 'hypothetico-deductive' methodology which emerged from the work of the Vienna Circle and American Pragmatists (Blaug 1992, Chapter 1). Abstract universal laws of economic behaviour are inferred and then the subsequent outcomes are painstakingly deduced with the strict rules of deductive logic. This stringent use of logic allows the neoclassical economist to create very complete mathematical models of economic relationships. The level of abstraction and mathematical power create models which can successfully execute their intended goal; namely, the prediction of *normal* economic events. The neoclassical theorists are not interested in explaining how a society's economic system came into existence (they begin from a predetermined general equilibrium situation) nor are they concerned with explaining all the intricacies of unusual behaviour. Their main goal is to be able to show how changes in system variables will influence the *normal* economic outcomes given the script imposed by their mathematical techniques.

It is not difficult to imagine the limitations of such a rigorous approach. There are many assumptions that reside within a model's basic structure that exist only to 'make the maths work'. For example, if one attempts to maximize or minimize a function that is not continuous (or well-behaved) the model immediately breaks down. To get around this, in elementary models, we assume that marginal utility is not discrete and factor inputs are easily divisible. In more advanced models, complex mathematics are employed to deal with step functions and the like but the result is always the same – additional limitations are being placed into the analysis that address only the method of analysis and not the economic phenomena under consideration. Simultaneous equations dictate that the researcher has the proper number of variables and equations. Traditional two-dimensional graphical analysis limits the use to two variables and evokes the insidious *ceteris paribus* assumption.

How this 'physics-mongering', to borrow a phrase from Phillip Mirowski (1989), came about is less important than seeing how the emulation of the physical sciences can actually hinder neoclassical economics' ability to examine economic phenomenon in any relevant manner. There is no question that this approach adds rigour to the science. Rigour, but as Heilbroner points out, 'rigor, but alas, also mortis' (Heilbroner 1970c, 2). The mathematical approach hamstrings the theorist so much that the construction of the abstract model itself becomes the goal. The researcher concentrates more on technique than economics. As a result models become elegantly constructed studies in sterility. Heilbroner states that:

> ...economists are apt to overlook that the powerful models of the physical science, which they seek to emulate, exist for one purpose only – to offer patterns of interdependence or hypothesized relation-

ships that can eventually be put to the test of empirical observation. That is, the main purpose of the model-building is to facilitate the eventual testing of the *premises* on which the models are constructed.... The controlled experiment that is the cornerstone of so much of physical science cannot be performed by the social scientist. Thus models of economic relationships proliferate endlessly because they are not subject to the constraints of application and practice that ultimately winnow the hypotheses of physical science. This is a condition which encourages the exercise of economic imagination for its own sake, with a concommitant indifference as to whether or not products explain or clarify the underlying social realities.

(Heilbroner 1970c, 4)

One of the greatest liabilities of this method is that social variables which are difficult to quantify or awkward to mathematically represent run the risk of being excluded. If the economist's famous tool kit does not include a technique for handling the particular social variable, then it is quite likely to be skipped. American hegemony in foreign trade, corporate power structures, pollution, changes in the institutional fabric are all critical to understanding the social order but all are conspicuously absent from the mainstream model. They are completely ignored or, perhaps worse, so dramatically simplified that they knowingly misrepresent the problem under consideration. Probably the most dangerous of these abstractions is the neoclassical construct of 'rational economic man'.

RATIONAL ECONOMIC MAN

Neoclassical economics is based on a highly individualistic (methodological individualism) approach to economic behaviour. Society is depicted as 'atomistic' in that the focus of analysis begins with the individual and is then summed to the collective. Using this technique, theorists cannot achieve any level of precision until they remove the inconsistencies in human behaviour. If, as I said earlier, the goal of the neoclassical theorist is to predict *normal* economic behaviour, then the first step in this process is to *normalize* human behaviour. By that I mean to remove the inconsistent (irrational) behavioural patterns and replace them with a more predictable and therefore modellable 'ideal human'. This ideal human has come to be known as *homo economicus* or rational economic man. Fundamentally:

Economic man (*homo economicus*) is an abstraction that defines the behaviour of humans in terms of an ideal type of rationality and thus of rational choice. The economic man always optimizes through rational choice and is never deflected from his goal by interests other than his own. (Canterbery 1995, 345)

Economic man provides the purified behaviour necessary for mathematical precision. Grounded in Bentham's hedonism and embodying marginalist's utility functions, economic man is seen to represent the basic human desire of always consistently operating in one's own self interest. As Adam Smith wrote more than two hundred years ago: 'It is not from the benevolence of the butcher, the brewer, or the baker, that we expect our dinner, but from their regard to their own self interest' (Smith 1776). For the neoclassical, individual optima are necessary for social optimum. Economic man consistently maximizes his pleasures and minimizes his pains to promote his own self-interest. By extension he can be seen to always maximize his profits and minimize his costs as well. Markets cease to allocate efficiently if all individuals in a given exchange transaction are not seen to be made better off. As long as individuals allocate their incomes, through the market, in ways which maximize their individual utility, all is well.

As a tool of abstraction *homo economicus* has been very successful. It does endow economic science with the internal stability its logical models require. It also removes many of the irrational aspects of individual behaviour which would naturally be nullified when society is taken as a whole. Many individual peccadilloes simply cancel each other when summed. Economic agents which systematically maximize and also minimize conveniently complement the extensive use of calculus in modern theory. Mathematical precision is achieved by bestowing behavioural patterns which are continuous, predictable and empirically verifiable. Predictable functions result in elegant curves and second order conditions determine if the individual has achieved a high or low point in their economic life. All of this is conducted in the name of economic science. A science that its practitioners would also like to be considered as being free of any value laden biases. Once the initial properties of economic man have been established, the science can determine various outcomes without fear of the researcher's personal agenda interfering with the results.

While economic science apes the physical science's hypothetico-deductive methodology, it differs in one very important way. Unlike the general laws of physical science, the laws of social science are not falsified if a single exception – Popperian falsification – proves them incorrect. In any given instance most would agree that a particular individual may deviate from their normal rational behaviour if faced with unusual or unfamiliar circumstances.

The abstracted 'ideal human' has not been without its critics. Many feel that human action is much too complex to be represented in such a limited fashion and to attempt to do so is an unconscionable simplification. It actually limits our understanding of any social question. If we know the behaviours before we begin then the results are theological. This concern with oversimplification is not a new development. In 1898 Thorstein Veblen redefined the concept of economic man as:

> The hedonistic conception of man is that of a lightening calculator of pleasures and pains, who oscillates like a homogeneous globule of desire of happiness under the impulsive stimuli that shift him about the area, but leave him intact.   (Veblen 1898)

While Veblen's remark is in his typical satirical tone, it does highlight the isolated character of the neoclassical approach. Neoclassical economics approaches from the viewpoint of a lone individual and not an individual within a social setting. Man is not seen as a social animal. This exclusion of the social dimension of individual behaviour is a keystone of Heilbroner's criticism of traditional economic theory.

I must point out that it is not the use of abstractions that Heilbroner finds troubling. The fact is he believes you can have no inquiry without abstraction. The problem lies in the construction of the abstractions. For example, if we return to the 'rational maximizing individual' of neoclassical theory, Heilbroner does not object to the terms rational or maximizing. These terms are useful as heuristics. What he does find objectionable is the third term, the 'individual'. Textbooks explain that the individual always allocates their income in ways which equalize the marginal utilities of the commodities consumed. However:

> ... *how does an 'individual' acquire an income, if not from another individual?* [italics in original] Does not the 'fundamental building block' thereupon become a dyad – a metaphor for society? Does this not remove all possibility of creating a study of economics from an individual, rather than from a social, starting point.
>
> (Heilbroner 1992a, 247)

This quotation highlights two distinct criticisms Heilbroner makes of traditional economics. To him, traditional economic science does not address the essential social dimension or the historical nature of true economic systems. For this reason, he has little use for general equilibrium models which can only be solved by assuming instantaneous adjustments. The market mechanism is a social construct which contains a collection of cultural and institutional elements such as social and political organization. These fundamental elements change through time. If economic science is to have relevance then it must account for this evolution. In other words, for Heilbroner, this removal of the social and historical aspects of human behaviour removes the ability to explain economic activity. In his words, 'conventional economics serves neither to depict accurately the structure or the tendencies of modern economic society, nor to guide reliably efforts to improve it' (Heilbroner 1970c, 1). Conventional economics, with its individualistic abstractions and formalistic methodology, becomes a veil which obscures our real understanding of economic provisioning.

The real question becomes how can economics be the science of individual economic behaviour when the individual is always embedded within a social system? If economics is to have any relevance, it must consciously model the system of which the individual is only a part. Social relations are more than a summation of individual relations. Adolph Lowe argues in his *On Economic Knowledge* (1965) that modern economic systems may lack the necessary *order* to be predictable. Further, this systemic *disorder* stems from social influences that shape the behaviour of individual economic agents. Lowe has been so influential to Heilbroner's thinking that I believe it is worth the time to understand the basics of his critique. We will see that many of Lowe's criticisms are often mirrored in Heilbroner's work as well.

ADOLPH LOWE'S CRITIQUE OF TRADITIONAL THEORY

Lowe argues that macroeconomic order – consistency in the overall functioning of the economy – can only be achieved if there is a minimum order among the micro-units (individual buyers and sellers) of the economy. That is to say that if the individuals within an economy act erratically then it is impossible to model the overall system. While neoclassical theorists assume this away in their primary construction of 'rational economic man', Lowe constructs a more complex theory of human behaviour. Lowe is not willing to brush aside possible causes of inconsistencies and simply assume rational maximizing behaviour. Lowe's model of 'micro-units' consists of observable *behavioural patterns* which rest upon a snetwork of individual *motivational patterns*. Within the motivational patterns are 'action directives' of the individual micro-units. These are defined as actions of purposive intent such as maximization and minimization of pecuniary profits and expenditures. These 'action directives' lie at the heart of the formal laws of supply and demand. This particular set of action directives have become known as the 'extremum principle'. For markets to operate, the individual *behavioural patterns* of buyers and sellers must intermesh smoothly. Buyers and sellers must find it advantageous to interact within a market setting and this is subject to the individual's motivational patterns. These motivational factors are subjected to a variety of influences. These influences can be intrasystemic (endogenous) or extrasystemic (exogenous). It is easy to imagine how extrasystemic motivations can influence individual behaviour. One only has to look to government regulations, supply shocks or unexpected changes in system components such as unexpected changes to the money supply. An economic environment which is undergoing external change is likely to show signs of disorderly behaviour. The interesting aspect is within the intrasystemic influence. Lowe asks if it is possible for motivational patterns to cause disorder even in a macroenvironment which is devoid of exogenous disruptions? This also includes individuals who always operate in their own self-interest and apply rational maximizing behaviour – consistent with their action directives. The answer Lowe offers is yes.

Lowe points to the role of expectations as a possible source of conflict.[3] He believes it is possible for individuals to operate in a maximizing manner (completely consistent with neoclassical assumptions) and still generate disorder in the macrosystem if expectations of the future differ from expected. He credits much of the conflict to what he calls changes in the 'economic time horizon'. He suggests that there are times when it may be rational for suppliers to withhold goods or services from the market. These would be times when they expect the price to increase in the future. If producers withhold goods from sale, even if buyers are willing to pay higher prices, then the fundamental law of supply is in jeopardy. It becomes possible to have a downward sloping supply curve. As prices increase, the quantity supplied is decreased. Two downward sloping curves may never intersect and therefore provide any sort of equilibrium condition. Markets simply may not clear. In other words, 'maximization has itself lost its classical determinacy, because the time span over which profits are to be max-imized can no longer be defined once and for all' (Lowe 1969, 12). In the nineteenth century when traditional economic laws were being formulated, individual behavioural patterns corresponded to the con-ventional maximizing norm. However, as the social order evolved, there has been several important changes.

First change was in capital formation. As mass production increased the development of capital formation, capital became less mobile. Capital was no longer able to be converted to interindustry production as easily as before. It took time to make the change. This modification in time constraint upset the traditional short-run focus. Firms could no longer react to changes in demand with the speed they once knew. Profit maximization was spread out over several time segments. This change in institutional structure does not violate the action directive of profit maximization; it simply alters the time horizon given the depth of capital structure in a given firm. Individual firms still maximized but their resulting behaviour depended on their depth of capital formation. It is possible to have several firms displaying different actions (beha-vioural patterns) even with identical motivational influences. The same can be said for the buyers' behaviour. As disposable income increased above subsistence levels, it may become rational for buyers to react to changes in price with changes in consumption. They still adhere to the action directive of the minimization of pecuniary expenditure, yet rational behaviour may differ if their levels of wealth differ. One individual may be forced to react strongly to price changes while others who have a greater surplus may react differently. As the economic time horizon expands, the traditional motivational patterns no longer pro-duce orderly behavioural patterns. The neoclassical model breaks down. The changes in the intrasystemic variables are influenced by the system-generated changes in institutional fabric which in turn changes the motivational patterns of the micro-units.

In all of Heilbroner's work there is some flavour provided by Lowe's political economy; as early as *Future as History* (1959) to *Visions* (1995) they all show considerable sensitivity to Lowe's work. Heil-broner's very definition of the role of economics carries a distinct influence of Lowe. Remember that Heilbroner does not define eco-nomics as the scarcity-based study of resource allocation. He believes that economics must be approached as 'a form of systematized power and of the socialized beliefs by which that power is depicted as a natural and necessary form of social life' (Heilbroner 1992a, 247). This is a very holistic and evolutionary definition of economics. His concern for how power is depicted as a natural form of social life is clearly Lowe's concern for intrasystemic influences – motivational patterns in particular. It is also clear from this definition that he, like Lowe, firmly places his economics within historical time.

FOUNDATIONS OF THE HEILBRONER CRITIQUE

Heilbroner argues that the social arrangements which economic science attempts to examine are the result of specific historical developments and are not attributes of society that are coexistent with humankind itself (Heilbroner 1987, 116). As I said earlier, market analysis is not of much use in examining premarket societies. Therefore, economics must be constructed so as to explain the economic behaviour during evolution of the social order. In Heilbroner's words, 'Once it is recognized that the research object of economics is intrinsically historical in its nature, any attempt to describe its fundamental elements shorn of this historical awareness can only obscure, rather than illuminate, its essential properties' (Heilbroner 1987, 116).

One way to illustrate how important social and historical factors are to Heilbroner's critique of traditional theory is to see what he finds wrong with traditional economic education. He questions whether students who are subjected to the study of marginal productivity, elasticities, and monetary theory are actually better off for the experience? Do our introductory economics classes actually help the student understand and deal with the economic realities with which they are faced? Heilbroner would argue that students would be better off if they understood size distribution of income, historical output trends and occupational changes more than the formula for determining arc elasticity. He somewhat tongue-in-cheek argues that: 'If I had my way, the introductory text for all beginning students would be the *Statistical Abstract*' (Heilbroner 1987, 119).

Heilbroner believes that economics should help the student understand our present economic situation *within* history. It must be able to answer questions such as: Where are we going? How did we get here? What has to change to get there? For economic pedagogies to be successful:

They must trace the rise of the market system from other integrative mechanisms – I would think that the middle portion of Karl

Polanyi's *The Great Transformation* would be required reading in
any introductory course. It is essential to show by concrete instance
that the economy, with its familiar behavioural ways, is an out-
growth of history, not an institution of unchanging human nature;
and that it will experience further historical change whose course is
difficult to foresee but is not, for that reason to be left unexamined.
                                                    (Heilbroner 1987, 119)

All of Heilbroner's criticisms that I have mentioned are valid concerns.
His insistence on historical and social relevance is a major contribution. However, nothing we have examined so far exemplifies the
true depth of his critique. Up to this point we see that Heilbroner's
dissension stems from his disagreements with the conscious methodological decisions made by neoclassical theorists. But this is only
half the picture. To fully appreciate this, we must move on to
his discussion of the role 'vision' and 'ideology' plays in economic
analysis.

ECONOMICS AS A VEIL

As we have seen, economic scientists strive to model and predict the
'behaviour' with the same detachment and stringent methods as their
natural science brethren. Natural scientists model the behaviour of
planets, molecules or elements while economists toil with human
economic behaviour. In an effort to produce 'value-free' results, economists diligently control the methods of data collection, statistical
testing and reporting with a devotion equal to that of the natural
scientist. However, all this care and mathematical precision cannot
overcome one substantial difference. The natural scientist enjoys an
inherent detachment from the phenomenon under examination. The
natural scientist's methods are analogous whether examining the
movement of planets or the movement of a compass needle as a
magnet is placed near it. The scientific method remains the same.
Economists, on the other hand, can never be quite as objective.
Regardless of the level of professionalism or control in experimental
design, it is a simple fact that the economic scientist is a *member* of the
group under study. Being part of the actual study in question places the
economist in a delicate position. It becomes difficult for the economist
to emulate the objectivity of the natural scientist. In Heilbroner's
words:

The economic investigator is in a fundamentally different relationship *vis-à-vis* his subject from that of the natural scientist, so that advocacy or value-laden interpretation becomes an inescapable part of social inquiry – indeed, a desirable part. (Heilbroner 1973, 130)

No matter how we try it is nearly impossible to achieve any truly 'value-free' analysis. All economic theory suffers from a degree of distortion caused by the 'vision' and 'ideology' of the investigating economist. This distortion is often ignored by the economics profession. If the distortion is not consciously recognized it becomes a 'veil' which ultimately denies us any true picture of our social system. For this reason, Heilbroner argues that economics should be approached as a 'belief system'.[4]

The approach to economics as a belief system is not as esoteric as it first may appear. All that is implied by the phrase is that economists should be aware that there are preconceptions and *a priori* moral implications embedded in their approach. For example, if capitalism is purely viewed as a market system, and the economist employs only market models in his analysis, then there may be critical aspects of the capitalist social order that will go undetected. It is not so much a question of competence of the inquirer as it is the proper make-up of the economist's famous tool kit. The application of pure market theory to modern capitalism may be akin to bringing a knife to a gunfight; it may be functional but perhaps not the most useful. It is more useful to see capitalism as a social order based on power as Heilbroner's definition of economics implies. The fundamental nature of capitalism may be the acquiescence of power, and the resulting price movements are purely an epiphenomenon (Stanfield 1995, Chapter 1). Heilbroner argues that the social dynamics that underpinned older societies may still exert their force in a modern market system. Concentrating only on the market process may 'throw a veil over other processes – a veil which obscures understandings and recognitions that, were they present, would cause 'economics' as well as market societies to look very different from the way they do (Heilbroner 1988a, 17). Therefore, Heilbroner's conception of economics as a system of power become clearer. He notes that:

The price system is also a system of power: that the work of analysis is inescapably colored by ideology and initiated by untestable 'visions'; that the object over which the veil is spread is not a collection of individuals but a specific social order to which we give the name capitalism.   (Heilbroner 1988a, 7–8)

'Vision' and 'ideology' are concepts which consistently prove very difficult to grasp. More often than not, the two are linked but never properly differentiated. Heilbroner follows the lead of Joseph Schumpeter in defining vision and ideology. Schumpeter (Schumpeter 1954, 41-2) defines vision as the 'pre-analytic cognitive act'. It is that which the researcher brings to analytic investigation. The personal bias or predetermined convictions which colour the researcher's original choice of what is of sufficient importance to be analysed.

Blatant ideology refers to the 'lying on behalf of an idea or an interest' (Heilbroner 1988a, 186). But not all ideology is blatant. What Heilbroner finds interesting is ideology which is of a more subtle form. It silently creeps into our analysis unwittingly. Let me offer an example from Heilbroner's *Behind the Veil*:

> Robert E. Lucas, a well-known conservative theorist, makes this reply to the question of whether governments do not try to resolve social injustice: 'That wouldn't be anything like my view. I can't think of explaining the pharaohs as being in existence to resolve the social injustice in Egypt. I think they perpetrated most of the injustice in Egypt.' The point at issue is not whether the pharaohs were, in fact, the perpetrators of most of the injustice in ancient Egypt, but why 'government' conjures up pharaonic Egypt for Lucas and not Lincolnian America. (Heilbroner 1988a, 188)

Lucas's conception of 'government' carries an unspoken indication of the ideological content of his work. It is not surprising that he would advocate limited government involvement when he likens all government to the pharaohs of ancient Egypt. I would seriously doubt that Lucas actually believes that American government can be couched in those terms, yet his economics would be consistent to this view. Much of this influence is transmitted through what E. D. Hirsch calls 'cultural literacy' (Hirsch 1988). Certain terms conjure up visions in the reader's mind and the truth or falseness of the argument is based on these visions.

While physical scientists are not completely exempt from the problems of 'vision' and 'ideology', they are somewhat shielded by the distance they are afforded from their work. Not being a member of the system under investigation gives them a distinct advantage over economists. Natural laws are constructed differently than economic laws. Returning to the compass and magnet example, Heilbroner states:

The natural scientist does not care about how his needle feels about magnetism, but the social scientist *has to know* how his buyers and sellers feel about the attraction of prices if his analysis is to be grounded on anything other than guesswork or blind faith.

(Heilbroner 1973, 136)

This close association to the subject matter and the interpretation of human intentions automatically injects an element of ideology and vision into all economic analysis. Sit through any session at the annual meetings of the American Economic Association and sooner or later you will invariably hear 'this may not be right but it is the best we have'. Traditional economists are fully aware of the limitations of their assumptions and method, yet they continue to act as if it were gospel. Why do economists continue to persist in their *mumpsimus*.[5] Why do they continue even when they know they are mistaken? As an example, why would economists continue to assume maximizing behaviour even if they know that this may not always be the truth? For Heilbroner the answer is simple. Economists must have some kind of assumptions about behaviour, and lacking anything better they continue to rest theory on an archaic maximization principle. If enough economists consistently state that more is better, then:

The idea of maximization thereby gives a certain 'scientific' authority to textbook statements that the consumer who climbs to the peak of his indifference map is more 'satisfied' than the one who camps like a vagabond, on some lower contour, or that an economy with a high growth rate is 'better off' than one with a lower rate. In a word, maximization becomes a prescription for conduct.

(Heilbroner 1973, 136–7)

This ideologically permeates throughout conventional theory because economists fail to realize that the essential terms in their vocabulary – wages, wealth, capital – are historical concepts which contain considerable sociopolitical implications. Conventional economists use these terms in their timeless and 'value-free' analysis and never acknowledge the social baggage this entails. A good example of this is the construction of the Robinson Crusoe economy to explain the 'rational' and 'maximizing' individual. As we saw earlier in this chapter, it is the term *individual* which Heilbroner finds to be lacking. In the Robinson Crusoe economy an individual cannot maximize their income as defined in the assumption of economic man. There is no income in this type of economy because income is essentially a social term. The individual could apportion his energy but 'energies are not income – if they were, all energetic individuals would be rich without further ado' (Heilbroner 1988a, 190). Income cannot be equated to economic provisioning in a one-person economy because income can only be derived from another individual. This could, of course, be made worse if, like many texts, we assume that individuals allocate their wages and thereby introduce a social hierarchy as well.

Given these concerns does Heilbroner believe we should abandon the emulation of the scientific method? Certainly not. He only hopes that economic science will realize the fact that there are some inherently sociopolitical elements in their approach. The seemingly 'objective' nature of traditional economic science can never scientifically 'disprove' the gradients of human behaviour in a particular social order. Economics must acknowledge that a social science is different from a natural science and the scientific method may obscure or veil the true question which needs to be answered. As Adolph Lowe argues:

> ...the interpretation of the ultimate 'facts' – buyers' and sellers' behaviour – by the actors themselves that so greatly encumbers the work of the economist, a difficulty which the student of molecules and planets, or of cells and organisms, is spared. (Lowe 1969, 5–6)

This chapter of criticisms and shortcomings leaves us with some serious questions. Is it possible to construct an economic science which can actually shed light on how a social order provisions for its material well-being? If all social inquiry is fraught with 'ideology' and a preconceived 'vision', is there any viable alternative to the mechanically complex yet behaviourally sterile neoclassical theory? The alternatives or solutions to these questions lie in the effort to emulate the *method* but not the *model* of the natural scientist. Heilbroner believes that there is an alternative methodology which incorporates into the analysis the advantages of an objective method while remaining inextricably linked to the dynamics of the social order. The method he advocates has become known as the method of *Worldly Philosophy*. The following chapter 'The Methodology of Worldly Philosophy' explores this 'worldly philosophy' and defines the essence of Heilbroner's socioeconomic inquiry.

4 The Methodology of Worldly Philosophy

Nothing comes closer to describing Robert Heilbroner's economic method than his own phrase *Worldly Philosophy*. It is remarkable that the title of his first book should remain the most lucid description of his 'economics' for over forty years. He has refined the content of his thought over the years but he has never questioned the broad scope of his initial inquiry. He simply paints on a much larger canvas than most economists. Heilbroner works in what has become known as the classical 'grand tradition' (Nell 1993b, 1). His scope is more inclusive than most modern economists. Market allocation is not the focus of his work although he admits that markets are inextricably linked to the capitalist social matrix. He is more interested in explaining the 'nature' and 'logic' of the social order than predicting simple price movements. This implies that he is specifically curious about the dynamics of the system. He wants to know how the system works and why it evolves as it does. Is it driven by some distinct 'human nature', or is it a combination of identifiable and predictable sociopolitical forces? This raises a question I have always found fascinating: Can economics be 'ism'[1] independent? In other words, is economic analysis unique to one particular social structure such as capitalism, socialism or feudalism? Do we need different economic models for every social structure, or is there some common element in all human behaviour which would explain material provisioning in a variety of societies? It should be noted that it would be easy to argue for independence if one were willing to accept a high enough level of abstraction. With sufficient boundary assumptions, neoclassical theory can explain anything from Caesar's Rome to the Robber Barons. The theory remains logically pure but the economics becomes intrinsically sterile: it tells us nothing of interest. Heilbroner writes: 'The 'high theorizing' of the present period attains a degree of unreality that can be matched only by medieval scholasticism' (Heilbroner and Milberg 1996, 4).

As this chapter unfolds, it will become apparent that Heilbroner's approach is decidedly eclectic. It does not fall within the bounds of any of the traditional schools of thought. It shares common features with many (Institutionalism, Marxism, Classical) but also contains sufficient differences to make any close association misleading. On the

37

surface one can observe it as a decidedly social analysis. It can also be seen to be firmly rooted in 'historical time' and not the 'logical time' which is the hallmark of the simultaneous equation approach of neo-classical theory. While his model is both 'logical' and 'scientific' – in the sense that it follows a distinct logical argument and employs rigorous analysis – it is not bounded by the strict 'positivist' methods that constrain most economic analysis. Heilbroner willingly strays into areas that most economists find taboo. He enters the realm of the sociologist, anthropologist and historian; sharing terminology, method and outlook. In the end, we will see that his aim is to provide a more comprehensive social *understanding* and not a prescriptive model of economic phenomena.

Before we delve into the complexities of the Heilbroner method proper, I believe it is useful to spend some time examining the economics of 'The Worldly Philosophers'. I begin this chapter with a brief look at what it takes to be considered a Worldly Philosopher. Specifically, I will look for any common elements that sets these men apart from others in the history of economic thought. Once this perspective is gained, we will be ready to progress to Heilbroner's model. We will see that Heilbroner's approach is really a tripartite solution. His approach contains three elemental components: elements of human behaviour, elements of socioanalysis and elements of economic modelling. Each of these work together to penetrate the veil of the social reproduction. The chapter concludes with a look at a selection of Heilbroner's policy prescriptions and social critiques so we can get a view of his model in action.

THE WORLDLY PHILOSOPHERS

In *The Worldly Philosophers*, Heilbroner gives us a glimpse of the lives and works of a very select group of economic scholars. The current edition of *The Worldly Philosophers* includes Smith, Malthus, Ricardo, Marx, Veblen, Keynes and Schumpeter. What distinguishes these men from others in their field is the rare curiosity they display about the social system as a whole. The worldly philosophers' 'economics' was not simple market dynamics. They understood that it is not possible to remove the economy from its surrounding social matrix. The two are inextricably linked. Market analysis may explain the mechanics of *how* scarce resources are allocated, but it lacks any power to discover *why* they are allocated. Therefore, the 'economics' of the worldly philo-

sophers goes beyond market analysis and seeks to explain the underlying, and often hidden, orchestrating forces of capitalism. In the end,
what they offer are large-scale scenarios of configurational change;
configurational change which alters social provisioning.

Heilbroner defines the essence of a worldly philosopher as 'the
search for the order and meaning of social history that lies at the
heart of economics' (Heilbroner 1953, 16). In other words, he asks:
'To what extent does economics enable us to perceive a structure
behind the confusion of daily life, a drama within the whirl of events?'
(Heilbroner 1953, 311). Perhaps the best way to understand the
worldly philosophy approach is to examine a short quote in which
Heilbroner describes the work of the first worldly philosopher, Adam
Smith. Heilbroner believes that Smith was the first to display a systematic attempt to explain the expansive 'nature and logic of capitalism'. He writes:

> He is a writer of political economy (the term 'economics' had not yet
> been invented) whose object of scrutiny was the social world in its
> widest dimensions and furthest reaches. Human nature, history,
> social psychology are the bedrocks on which his architecture of
> ideas was raised; and although his conclusions about mankind are
> profoundly conservative, we shall soon discover that his enormous
> authority resides, in the end, in the same property that we discover in
> Marx: not in any ideology, but in an effort to see to the bottom of
> things. In both cases, their greatness rests on an unflinching con-
> frontation with the human condition as they could best make it out.
> (Heilbroner 1986, 1)

I should point out that the label, worldly philosopher, is not intended
to imply that all these scholars had similar views on economic activity.
Marx's 'mature communism' is clearly a very different destination from
Smith's 'society of perfect liberty'. The worldly philosopher label
intends neither to give insight into the scholars' personal character or
their political views. What it does provide is a very broad category into
which we can place these men without the didactic constrictions of
typical schools of thought. The work of worldly philosophers actually
forms the foundation of many of the traditional schools of thought;
therefore, such categorization is meaningless. The group is too diverse.
In fact the diversity of this group is one of its most interesting
characteristics. Heilbroner writes: 'There were among them a philosopher, and a madman, a cleric and stockbroker, a skeptic and a

tramp. They were from every walk of life, of every turn of temperament. Some brilliant, some bores; some ingratiating, some impossible' (Heilbroner 1953, 15). While each man was unique, there is one thing they all share. They all 'sought to embrace in a scheme of philosophy the most worldly of all of man's activities – his drive for wealth' (Heilbroner 1953, 16).

All of the worldly philosophers approach their work with an economic vision that few modern economists can comprehend. Today Nobel Prizes are awarded for adding to the economist's famous tool kit. Game theory, statistical expectation models and mathematical expressions are all the rage. It would be interesting to see what the worldly philosophers think of their profession today. Here is a group of scholars whose work provides the very foundations of the science but, for the most part, would be considered too unsophisticated in modern terms. I doubt that any referee for the *American Economic Review* could recommend anything that was submitted (blindly of course) by the members of the group. The comments would surely be 'too broad', 'lacks focus', 'add rigour.' But it is for these reasons that the worldly philosophers were so important. Today economic technicians narrowly write for their colleagues. In fact, it is only other economists who have the sufficient training to understand the majority of the arguments. Gone are the days when laymen could extract useful guidance from the profession's top journals. Today economics is written in very precise code. Articles are focused on very minute problems or provide extensions to previous models. The journals are nothing more than very exclusive clubs. Admission is limited to those who possess the required expertise and have invested the necessary time in the history of the particular journal. Articles are episodic serials in a continuing story of the journal's subdiscipline. It is easy to imagine Adam Smith absentent-mindedly thumbing through the *AER* and asking why? Why is this useful? Why are modern economists so fascinated with precision when they freely admit that their models rest upon a platform of simple abstractions which are centuries old? We don't know the fundamentals of human provisioning and yet we accept or reject a model if it lacks the sufficient number of decimal points. This almost common sense approach to economics is nearly extinct.

Before we go much further it may be useful to list a few defining characteristics of the worldly philosopher group. First, as I stated earlier, each man was interested in explaining the social system as a whole. What they designed were not reductionist models. Each was a comprehensive model which today would stray into the related fields of history, sociology and psychology. The worldly philosophers designed systematic, integrated and interrelated models of human provisioning. None of the worldly philosophers were content to provide only a piece of the puzzle; they offered comprehensive solutions. This is probably the reason why so many automatically link their work with Newtonian or 'natural order' modelling. This type of association is correct if we think of Newtonian modelling as being the doctrine of scientific determinism. That is, the principle that all events are the inescapable result of preceding causes (Canterbery 1987). If you look at the work of Smith, Marx or Keynes one begins to see that each man makes assumptions about human nature and the society's institutional structure, and then extrapolates the system's future. Each scenario is deduced through a logical chain of cause and effect. The system unfolds through the endogenous interaction of the reasoned variables. What sets the worldly philosophers apart is the range of variables they were willing to view as endogenous. In other words, the scope of their vision. The worldly philosophers specifically incorporated sociopolitical variables into their economics. Smith, for example, blended social laws with his economic laws of human behaviour. He fused the political liberalism of Locke with his own economic liberalism to provide the genesis of his analysis of early capitalism. He coupled market analysis with a much larger social analysis to form his economics. This same breadth of vision can be seen in the work of all the worldly philosophers. In fact, most of the scenarios, from Smith to Keynes, were based on the same maximizing behaviour assumption as modern economic models. However, the worldly philosophy scenarios specifically included political and institutional structures which are lacking in current models. If we read between the lines of the worldly philosophy group, we find a chronicle of a member or class of society. It is a narrative of the agents' troubles, adversaries, work and their potential destination. In Smith, Ricardo, Mill and Marx the chronicle is about the changing outlook for the social order itself, changes in relative class divisions being paramount. A little later, Marshall and Keynes focused on a faceless group of 'individuals' and their related income distributions. Their choice of principal agents (initial vision) gives the best indication of their true intention. Understanding their initial focus can tell us more about their true beliefs than any anthology of their work.

The second distinguishing characteristic of the worldly philosophy group is their desire to use their work to affect social change. No member of the group was willing to simply espouse his ideas. Each wanted to see their work in action. Heilbroner writes:

> It is not one of their flaws, but one of their claims to greatness as economists that Smith, Ricardo, Mill, Marx, Marshall, and Keynes were explicit in their use of facts and theories as instruments of advocacy. Smith's great model of the economic system was written not merely to 'analyze the late eighteenth-century England, but to plead for a policy of 'perfect liberty' and to assail the policies of mercantilism.   (Heilbroner 1973, 139–40)

Mill and Ricardo's Parliament service; Keynes representing Britain at Bretton Woods, and at the Council of Four in 1919;[2] Marx's substantial involvement in the Internationals, are all examples of these men using their economics to change their social world.

The third distinguishing characteristic is so obvious that it is often dismissed. The third characteristic is the conspicuous fact that all these men were economists. This means that each thought that economic analysis was the proper vehicle for social understanding. For these men, economic activity is the underpinning of all social activity. In times when tradition and custom dictated how a society provisions, economics is irrelevant. The study of economics would add nothing if we already had a complete picture of a 'traditional' society's cultural mores and technologies. The motives and pressures of tradition orchestrate production and distribution. There are no separate 'economic' incentives. The same would hold true for command and kingship societies. Once the political power structure is understood, economic science adds little value. Again, a thorough understanding of the political, technological and cultural structures of a command system leaves little for the economist to discover. The provisioning is so completely integrated with the command structure that it is all that is required to explain the system. Economics is simply not necessary. This is not to say that there was no 'economic' activity in these types of societies. That is certainly not the case. Any society has some organizational function which facilitates production and distribution. In tradition and command systems this 'economic' activity is so intermeshed with the political or cultural attributes of the society that no separate economic analysis is needed. It is only in capitalist societies that distinctly separate 'economic' motivations begin to appear. These motivations are separate from political and cultural attributes. The motivations are economic and therefore fall to economic science to explore. They may exist in conjunction with political and cultural criteria but they are unique enough to require a separate form of inquiry. It should then come as no surprise that all the great economic philosophers were working in capitalist systems. Only in a capitalist structure does economics really have any intrinsic value. For economics to be central to social understanding, economic motivations must provide the primary dynamic to the system.

THE DOMINANT SOCIAL ORDER

As we move into the twenty-first century, capitalism will certainly be the dominant social order. Even though capitalism will survive, those familiar with Heilbroner's work will know that he has some reservations about the future of worldly philosophy. He has questioned on several occasions (Heilbroner 1953, Heilbroner 1992b) whether this approach will be compatible with modern capitalist systems. This is a serious consideration since we have begun to classify Heilbroner himself as working in the 'worldly philosophy' tradition.

Heilbroner has two main concerns about the future of worldly philosophy. His first is the disturbing trend in modern economic science toward reductionist modelling. The more comprehensive worldly philosophy approach does not mesh with the quantitative methods of modern mainstream thought. Today economists avoid any model of large-scale configurational change 'because it lends itself poorly to the procedures of formal analysis' (Heilbroner 1992b, 374). The modern economist's desire to be 'scientific' has led the profession down a narrow path where only those variables that conveniently fit the meticulous chains of logic are included. Although the heterodox economists in the institutionalist approach seem to be consistent with the worldly philosophy approach, the sociopolitical dimension has been effectively purged from mainstream theory.[3] In most economic modelling, the web of social relationships is abstracted to a point where they cease to be valuable. These difficult social aspects have been relegated to economics' sister disciplines such as sociology and political science. Heilbroner writes:

> Politics and sociology – and beneath them, psychology in all its forms – do not possess the lawlike regularities of behaviour that demarcate economics as a field of social analysis, investing it uniquely with the characteristics of a social science... In no way

does this difference make economics prior to, or deeper than, its neighboring approaches, but it does endow it with the capability of developing causal sequences that are often their envy and despair.
(Heilbroner and Milberg 1996, 5)

These related fields employ methodologies which are unfamiliar to most traditional theorists. This shifting focus does not by itself rule out the possibility of larger-scale social inquiries. However, finding qualified economists who also embody the requisite skills and courage to cross their discipline's borders does make us question the future of worldly philosophy. Many of the younger economists are drawn to the profession because of its quantitative qualities. To change their focus could not guarantee their proficiency in the more inclusive field. In fact, following their own argument – labour markets efficiently allocating skills – makes this somewhat unlikely; the profession gets what its majority wants.

Heilbroner's second concern for the future of worldly philosophy is more disturbing. He submits that the worldly philosophy approach may be condemned because of the more political nature of contemporary economic life. He writes that the 'government is now inextricably entwined in the outcome of the economic process, introducing a crucial element of political determinism into the course of economic life'(Heilbroner 1992b, 374). In other words, the path of the economy is no longer determined exclusively by the actions of the economic agents. If the production and distribution are orchestrated by something other than capitalist motives, economics may be of little use. This argument is best presented in his entry in Philip Arestis and Malcolm Sawyer's *A Biographical Dictionary of Dissenting Economists*. Heilbroner writes:

I have come to doubt that the historic course of contemporary capitalism can be depicted in terms of a self-regulating socioeconomic drama. For reasons of institutional size and complexity, changes in social attitudes and ever-more-urgent political imperatives, all capitalist economies are today subject to political direction of one sort or another, including the very important political decision as to the areas in which, and the extent to which, market processes will be allowed to work their way unhindered. This is a setting so different from that of the past as to make the purely economic scenarios of the classical thinkers largely irrelevant.
(Heilbroner 1992a, 243)

This wavering belief in modern worldly philosophy can be traced to Adolf Lowe's (Lowe 1965) diagnosis of the breakdown in economic order. Like Lowe, Heilbroner is beginning to question if contemporary capitalism can be depicted in terms of a self-regulating socioeconomic order. Using Lowe's terminology, contemporary capitalism may lack the sufficient *behavioural* and *motivational* patterns necessary to establish macro-order. If these patterns are absent, activity may be sliding toward the opposite end (disorder) of the spectrum. Effective explanation and prediction of this order requires economic models which are fluent in the *predictable* laws of the underlying agent's psychology. These behavioural laws need not accurately depict all human behaviour in all circumstances. All that is required is they infer general order on the system.

For example, the classical assumption of maximizing behaviour did not enjoy such an extended success because economic agents really 'maximized' in every economic decision. No, all that is required for the system to function is that the agents act *as if they maximized*. The behaviour of any individual in society displayed enough consistency that the other people were able to consistently predict the actions of others. People consistently maximized profits by bringing goods to market. Others provided the necessary transportation and support services necessary for the system to function. Expectations were generated based on a set of traditional behaviours sufficient to produce a narrow enough band of actions to be fundamentally predictable. The system worked because everyone knew the rules.

Today institutional structures do not yield the same consistency. Increased personal wealth allows speculating behaviour which may keep goods off the market for long periods of time. In the era when the worldly philosophers worked, expectations and actions were consistent with the classical postulates and economic order was easier to explain. As Adolph Lowe wrote in 1935:

> The whole idea of an autonomous economic science can only arise, if there are 'economic' elements in human behavior which are not necessarily 'social' elements at the same time, that is to say, which do not necessarily relate to a plurality of persons, a human group.
>
> (Lowe 1935, 41–2)

If future capitalist systems become, as Heilbroner projects, so completely infused with political activity, then application of current economic theory may not yield useful scenarios. We may no longer have 'social dramatists who dare to base such large-scale narratives on so narrow a motivational base' (Heilbroner 1953, 324). The reign of the worldly philosopher as we know it may indeed be over.

The era of the worldly philosophers may have passed. It may no longer be possible to approach the complexities of modern life armed only with the economist's tool kit. Their models may become only pages of the history of economic thought but their influence will surely continue to inspire. Heilbroner knows these men taught us a great lesson. His parting words in the latest edition of *The Worldly Philosophers* are:

> As few other thinkers, the worldly philosophers taught us to see the evolution of society as a drama whose meaning could be grasped by individuals who would otherwise have felt themselves merely swept along by overmastering and incomprehensible forces. The ultimate objective of their economic thinking was social understanding. That extraordinary lesson for human emancipation will not be forgotten. (Heilbroner 1953, 325)

The worldly philosophers' models may be antiquated, but their *vision* does not have to fade. The initial breath of their research is what made economic science useful. It provided the start of the field. In modern economics there is, of course, room for the technicians, the number tumblers who give us our scientific aura. However, there must also be a segment of the profession who are willing to apply the profession's output to relevant social problems. Elegant models which do not aid social understanding are mere ornamentations.

This brings us to the question: Is Heilbroner a worldly philosopher? I believe the answer is yes. He consistently criticizes the mainstream for its narrow formalist tendencies, hoping to bring back the missing sociopolitical dimension in economics. The ultimate proof is of course the calibre of Heilbroner's economics. Does he offer an alternative that is consistent with modern capitalist structures that can ultimately uphold the fundamental vision and spirit of the worldly philosophers. Is his economics penetrating enough to illuminate the economic structure behind everyday life?

HEILBRONER'S SOCIOPOLITICAL ECONOMICS

A quick glance through Heilbroner's book titles tells us his approach is different from most economists. Titles like *An Inquiry Into the Human*

Prospect, The Future as History, Behind the Veil of Economics, Visions of the Future, and *The Making of Economic Society* provide a strong indication of the breadth of Heilbroner's vision. These titles are not the standard fare of a traditional economist. This focus is more reminiscent of what we have just seen from his worldly philosophers. Edward Nell, Heilbroner's longtime colleague at the New School for Social Research, argues that Heilbroner should not only be included within the older classical 'grand tradition', but that he is actively expanding and developing this method (Nell 1993b). We will see the expansion to which Nell refers, is directed at Heilbroner's uncertainty for the future of worldly philosophy. Heilbroner continues the classical tradition but with an acute consciousness of the evolving nature of economic systems. Nell places his colleague squarely in the classical tradition, however:

> ... unlike many of the classics, and especially unlike some of their modern followers, he sees the patterns of development of different social formations as unique to each. General laws of development, transcending social formations, are not to be found. Ancient society, feudalism and capitalism each develop according to their own logic, the study of which is the proper basis of economic analysis.... (Nell 1993b, 6)

Nell paints a picture of economic modelling that has a distinctly historical composition. He sees the need for a different set of judgement criteria for each economic epoch. In this I believe he is not mistaken. Each social formation does have its own character just as Baroque differs from Rococo and Modernist. Using a common set of merit criteria for each historical period would place more emphasis on the criteria than the subject under consideration. Didactic techniques should reflect relevant social interaction much the same as Leonardo's dictum of mirrors reflects artistic acuity[4] (Gardner 1975). Perceptive economic analysis operates on multiple and often interlocking levels. Simple market analysis provides answers to transactional mechanics but it lacks the scope necessary to penetrate the sociopolitical complexities of modern capitalism. Market analysis concentrates on surface economics and therefore becomes a *veil* to underlying economic forces. We have to look behind or beneath traditional analysis if we want to understand the complexities of the social order. Modern capitalism is a system of power structures, social interactions, institutional formations and structures of distributional mechanisms. But even beneath this, economic provisioning rests on a bedrock of human nature. Nell continues:

> For the nature and logic of social formations must be grounded in something. Part of the answer will be found in environment... but the environment is simply there: to shape the formation of a society it has to enter the actions and reactions of people. Hence the other and more significant term of the relationship is that elusive philosopher's stone, social thought, 'human nature'.   (Nell 1993b, 6)

Heilbroner was certainly not the first to be concerned with human nature in economics. Smith's human behavioural generalizations which include the propensity to 'truck, barter and exchange'; Keynes's 'animal spirits'; Marx's motivations of the bourgeoisie all addressed this elusive human mystery. Heilbroner believes if we can effectively confront this basic human essence we may get a glimpse of the true science of provisioning.[5]

We have now gained a substantial flavour of Heilbronerian economics. Heilbroner's work is difficult to categorize. He cannot be said to work fully in one traditional school. Readers in search of stylized axioms and econocentric jargon will likely be disappointed. Detailed graphical and mathematical rigour is also conspicuously absent. His work is rigorous but in ways which differ from traditional economics. He is not an empirical economist, methodological positivist or complete relativist. His association to worldly philosophy conjures up a certain image, but it contains many vagaries and unexplained nuances. For example, we know from the previous chapter what Heilbroner considers to be a veil in mainstream thought. We have seen that he incorporates the basics of human nature into his economics. We have completed a long journey around the perimeter of his work, but this I believe is necessary to comprehend Heilbroner's economics on all its levels. I now believe we have reached a point where we can appreciate a formal presentation of his economics. In the following section, I will organize the material as he would when considering another economist: vision, approach and method, and formal structure of the model.

HEILBRONER'S VISION

Robert Heilbroner's fundamental vision is the inherently sociopolitical nature of economic analysis. Just as Joseph Schumpeter's *elites* were never far from his work, Heilbroner's sensitivity to the political nature of economic life is a constant companion. On the rare occasions when he is speaking directly of his vision he states:

> I hope in a fashion that [my vision] has been explicit from the start – namely, that economics is inextricably sociopolitical in nature... I further believe that the sociopolitical aspect of economics applies in particular – perhaps even exclusively – to social orders whose economies manifest three properties: they are driven by a restless desire to accumulate capital, knit together by largely unregulated markets, divided into two realms, one private and one public. In a word, they are modern capitalist societies.   (Heilbroner 1996, 334)

As we have just seen, Heilbroner strongly believes that addressing the sociopolitical aspects in economic activity is vital to its understanding. Furthermore, his economics, like the worldly philosophers before him, is consciously directed toward capitalist economies. As we will see in the next chapter, the defining characteristics of a capitalist system include the existence of markets, the drive to accumulate capital, and the division of power between public and private realms. His *vision* forces his 'economics' to directly confront each of these properties. In other words, his economics is the conscious study of capitalist systems. For this reason I will spend the next few chapters detailing the particulars of his view of the capitalist order. In the meantime, with the elusive properties of vision behind us we can move on to his approach and methodology.

HERMENEUTIC METHOD

Most economists conduct their analysis with the strict discipline imposed by the modern hypothetico-deductive approach (Blaug 1992). This methodology with its symmetry thesis, logical falsification and formalized positivist structures employs the framework necessary for accepted scientific progression. A scientific analysis whose specific purpose is prediction (to a lesser extent explanation) of the phenomena under consideration. Positivist methods allow us to induce general behavioural laws and then deduce situations from A to B to C within a repeatable chain of causation. One problem with most positivist theory is once the preliminary laws are induced, they are seldom questioned. These laws become givens and are pushed to the background. Questions in economic methodology typically focus on elements below the behavioural law. Most consideration is given to the agent in question – individualist or collectivist (part of the social whole). In economics, the hypothetico-deductive approach is taken for granted; positivist methods predominate.

Heilbroner, on the other hand, works somewhat outside this style as he does not employ a traditional positivist methodology. This often makes his work misunderstood by those expecting traditional fundamentals. What typifies his work is the goal of a general understanding of the aspect in question and not desire for a straight prediction. This allows him to pose questions without the ultimate purpose of empirical justification. Data collection or mining is his concern. Under the tutelage of Adolph Lowe, he began to develop a more inclusive method of inquiry. He writes:

> I began to see economics as something other than the analysis of a wholly unambiguous object of investigation called 'economic reality'. In its place emerged the problem of identifying an 'economy' within the totality of perceived social relations – an act that determined both the boundaries of the object to be studied and the constitutive elements of the discipline that studied it. Although I do not think I knew the word, I was thus oriented towards what has come to be known as a hermeneutic, as opposed to a positive, approach to economic inquiry.   (Heilbroner 1992a, 242)

The first question which comes to mind is what exactly is *hermeneutic*? Unfortunately, hermeneutics seems to be one of those terms like postmodernist: it can be all things to all people. While the term may not have a single definitive meaning, we certainly can decipher a sufficiently broad understanding of the concept. For our purpose, we can 'view hermeneutics as a type of philosophical activity or praxis, the effort to understand what is distant in time and culture... or obscured by ideology or false consciousness' (Shapiro and Sica 1984). According to Shapiro and Sica, the ultimate 'hermeneutical aim is to make such understanding meaningful for life and thought' (Shapiro and Sica 1984). Another scholar working in the hermeneutical tradition, Brice Wachterhauser, believes that 'hermeneutical theories of understanding argue that all human understanding is never 'without words' and never 'outside of time' (Wachterhauser 1986, 5). This fits well with Heilbroner's advocation of 'historical time' (not logical time) as well as his concern for recognizing the moral and ethical content of economic jargon. Hermeneutics has another facet which may be useful in understanding Heilbroner's work. It is the capacity of human beings to be aware of their past. Sociologist Anthony Giddens explains:

> For hermeneutic authors history – not as the elapsing of time but as the capability of human beings to become aware of their own past and to incorporate that awareness as part of what their history is – has always been at the center of the social science.
>
> (Giddens 1984, 219)

Like Giddens, Heilbroner is very perceptive of the changing nature of social interactions and institutional formations. In fact one key characteristic of Heilbroner's economics is the belief that economic analysis cannot exist as some kind of socially disembodied study (Heilbroner and Milberg 1996, 6). Human nature cannot be replicated with the precision of physical laws of the natural sciences. A further complication is the fact that the economist is actually part of the social unit under examination. Hermeneutic methodology allows Heilbroner to enter questions of morality, ideology and social consciousness into his work. Where typical economics wishes to purge these aspects from its inquiry, Heilbroner exploits them. He actively examines the meaning of the terminology and ideology of economic science. They provide a more subtle strata to his modelling.

Positivist creations of science emphasize the anchoring of their theories in observation statements, hypotheses, verification and prediction of the logical components of their model. I want to emphasize that Heilbroner's economics does employ rigorous analysis. He is adamant about 'attending scrupulously to chains of reasoning, and of guarding against the always present temptation to submit to demagoguery for intellectual exchange' (Heilbroner and Milberg 1996, 4). His analysis is simply more multifaceted than traditional economic science. Hermeneutics in Heilbroner's hands is an interpretation of social history. The subtleties of this approach will become more apparent in the following chapter on capitalism. Approaching capitalism as a regime or gestalt is where the flexibility of a hermeneutic approach comes into its own. Meanwhile, it is now time to turn our attention to a more formal presentation of Heilbroner's model. We know that his *vision* of the sociopolitical content of economics is always directing his work. We also know that this vision is directed through a hermeneutic and not a positivist method of inquiry. We now will see the superstructure of his method, the formal structure of his model.

FORMAL STRUCTURE OF HEILBRONER'S MODEL

As I described in the introduction of this chapter, Heilbroner's model combines elements of human behaviour, socioanalysis, as well as more formal elements of economic modelling; each element building upon the other to provide a multilayered social theory; each component as important as the other and each supporting the other two. Human biological and psychological characteristics give rise to, and are shaped by, social interaction. These larger social forces then determine the production and distributional formations of economic systems. To understand the total effect of the model's ability, it must be coupled with Heilbroner's view of capitalism which is the subject of the next chapter. However, at this point we can gain a fundamental understanding of each of the model's components.

The Human Element

To understand human provisioning, we must go beneath market analysis to the human agents of the market. While Heilbroner is the first to admit that we have no plausible complete theory of human behaviour (Heilbroner 1975, 416), the element of human understanding is paramount. It is true that we have no model in the social sciences which has the sufficient power to consistently predict human action. However, this does not mean we cannot obtain some understanding of human behaviour. This *hermeneutic* understanding can direct our inquiries. In the study of economic systems, we must first decipher the human traits which allow sufficient *order* in human behaviour for a complex institution like the market to operate.[6] In cultures where tradition or command control the generation and distribution of goods, this inherent order still exists. Karl Polanyi talks about the acts of production and distribution (economics) as being 'embedded in non-economic institution' (Polanyi 1968, 86) . This implies the necessary forms of social production are 'dispatched' in accordance with social obligation. While this is true, it does not get to the root of the human condition. What we need is an examination of the motivations of Polanyi's acts (Heilbroner 1988a, 18). We need to understand the basic motivations which allow humans willingly to become part of the social whole. Most modern economists treat human economic agents as completely individual units. Heilbroner, on the other hand, begins his analysis by looking at why humans act within the order-bestowing mechanisms of kinship, reciprocity and duty. He wants to know what is fundamental to human experience which would allow their socialization into any form of economic system. He questions:

> The ability to behave in 'adult' fashion, including the performance of socially designed roles, must in every society be traced back to the behavior-shaping process of socialization, in particular the prolonged nurturant experience in which the psychological and biological givens of the human species-beings are gradually given socially acceptable shape and form.   (Heilbroner 1988a, 18)

To examine this he takes his lead from depth psychology and psychological anthropology. He believes the inescapable socialization process is in part due to 'affect'.[7] He writes:

> It is 'affect' that permits or encourages or even demands the cooperative association of individuals, and that makes the assumption of some form of interindividual, rather than autistic behavior, a necessary starting point for all social analysis.   (Heilbroner 1988a, 19)

Affect provides only a portion of the answer. We still need to explain away fundamental human obedience and acquiescence. Why in a contemporary society like twentieth-century America, with its grandiose vision of individual culture, do people willingly become subservient to an invisible institution like the market? Why do they display sufficient reciprocity and truth to make the system work? Heilbroner writes:

> Those traits also depend on the socialization process, where they emerge from the gradual acceptance and internalization of the parental frustration imposed on infants' and childrens' fantasies and drives. However sympathetically this frustration is imposed, it is universally present in the nurturant experience, where it becomes internalized and sublimated to form the basis for adult obedience and – as the delayed enactment of repressed infantile fantasies – for the pleasures of adult domination.   (Heilbroner 1988a, 19)

This combination of affect and acquiescence to authority then can be seen to orchestrate 'order' in any number of economic orders. Tradition, command or market economies rest on this fundamental human propensity for social interaction.

As I said earlier, Heilbroner admits that we do not have fully predictive models of human behaviour. However, he does believe that Marxism and psychoanalysis provide the closest alternative.

This type of psychological approach is helpful in explaining behaviour in a number of historical trends. He writes:

> ...I believe it is fair to claim that psychoanalysis and Marxism are today the leading contenders for a holistic approach to the problem of behavior; and I think that it can be shown that within each discipline there exists a pattern of inquiry and set of basic postulates sufficiently well defined to enable us to speak generally of a 'Marxist' and 'psychoanalytic' interpretation of behavior despite the spectrum of interpretations that flourishes in each camp.
>
> (Heilbroner 1975, 418)

Similar concerns to understanding human behaviour can be seen in historian Peter Gay's work (Gay 1985.) He argues that the 'professional historian has always been a psychologist' (Gay 1985, 6). While it is true 'you can psychoanalyze the dead' common behavioural patterns are present in every epoch. Marx utilized this to explain his materialist view of history. We will see this Marxist sympathy is a common thread to all Heilbroner's economics; it blends well with the *hermeneutic* understanding approach. This is because Heilbroner views Marxism as a 'diagnostic' discipline. The *diagnosis* (understanding) is the first step towards a therapy (policy). We must first understand or at least acknowledge before we can proceed with a social prescription. This Marxist influence continues into the second tier or level of Heilbroner's model. Marx's socioanalysis is the foundation upon which Heilbroner rests his social inquiry.

Sociopolitical Analysis

Humans are social creatures or 'herd animals' to borrow a term from Marx. Therefore, an individual's behavioural patterns are influenced by the surrounding environment and the individual in turn influences that environment. It is a continual interaction and reinforcement process. Marx attempted to explain these underlying social currents with what he termed 'socioanalysis'. In *Marxism: For and Against*, Heilbroner writes: 'Marx's socioanalysis tries to penetrate the surface appearances of the system and to unveil its concealed essence' (Heilbroner 1980, 61). We should by now expect this type of declaration from Heilbroner. It has the exact same focus as his *hermeneutic* approach to economics. It repeats his main question: What lies under the surface of economic society? That is the central question Heilbroner addresses. It is, of course, the same definition he gives to *worldly philosophy*. The socioanalysis of Marxism runs deeply throughout all of Heilbroner's economics. Heilbroner believes:

> The socioanalysis of the system, starting with the lowly commodity that contains within itself the disguised elements of the class struggle, strikes me as one of the most extraordinary and illuminating acts of intellectual penetration of which we have record, truly meriting the comparison I have so often drawn with Plato and Freud. That penetrative capability is the unique, and, I think the most remarkable and enduring, achievement of Marxism. It opens an understanding of society that is otherwise totally inaccessible, giving us the opportunity to grasp what we are, the necessary precondition of knowing what we might become. (Heilbroner 1980, 137–8)

It is difficult to find higher praise of a single idea. Marx's socioanalysis is clearly a defining characteristic of Heilbroner's economics. His economics has the single purpose of explaining the social order called capitalism.

Heilbroner defines socioanalysis as 'the historically oriented, dialectically based dissection of the particular institutions and beliefs of capitalism' (Heilbroner 1980, 94). Heilbroner's view of capitalism as more than a market system is fundamental to his model. Power in a capitalist system is separated into public (political) and private (economic) realms. Power in the private or economic realm is divided into class boundaries and a dialectic method is useful in explaining its internal tensions. Heilbroner believes that any economic analysis must include this social dimension of power.

As we move to the more technical aspects of the Heilbroner economic theory, it is critical that we keep in mind that it is first and foremost a model of *social* provisioning. The sociopolitical element cannot be separated from the economic. The social is built upon, and shaped by, the understanding of the human behavioural. The economic or *provisioning* element is then the natural outcome of the other two. Separation is not possible. Economists cannot construct a 'socially disembodied' model.

Economic Theory

In Chapter 2 we saw that Heilbroner defines economics as the study of the systematized power and socialized beliefs. This power and social organization is different in command, tradition or market economies. We also know that Heilbroner believes that only capitalist systems display the materialistic behavioural patterns which warrant economic analysis. Therefore, we cannot fully understand his economics without moving on to a more thorough discussion of capitalism. However, because Heilbroner does not erect anything resembling a formal supply–demand type of economic model, we must first briefly identify any important institutional 'elements' of his system. Elements such as production and distribution technologies, externalities and class relations.

The list of economic topics is endless but the heart of economics is always the same. Heilbroner writes:

> One can investigate literally hundreds of economic problems, but ultimately one is always investigating a single problem – *the* economic problem of how men sustain themselves in the face of recalcitrant nature and a still more recalcitrant human nature.
>
> (Heilbroner 1995, 30)

For Heilbroner, the fundamental economic problem – mankind's material provisioning – is not scarcity-based. To Heilbroner, 'the scarcity of nature only sets the stage' (Heilbroner 1995, 3). Nature may not offer its resources in such abundance that man can live without making allocating decisions. The immediate enemy in sustaining sufficient provision is man himself – economic scarcity is manmade.

Primitive man lived in a state of relative satiety coupled, of course, by periods of great privation and suffering. Modern man, economists tell us, now lives in a world of scarce resources and unlimited wants. The question interesting to Heilbroner is: 'What is the source of this insatiable commodity-hunger that we discover in adult man but not in his infancy?' (Heilbroner 1987, 112). Where did this come from? When did nature become so stingy or humans so greedy? Heilbroner wants to explore the reasons for this fundamental change in the human condition. This has been a fundamental element to his economics since the beginning. In 1963 he wrote:

> When, in 1933, one working American out of four was unable to find a job – even though empty factories virtually begged to be set running again – it was not nature which posed the economic crisis, but man.
>
> (Heilbroner 1963c, 3)

This brings us full circle to the beginning of his methodology of *Worldly Philosophy*. The solution to the economic problem does not reside in a complex economic model. It can only be found in a carefully conducted, historically oriented, social inquiry. An inquiry which employs his triad of understandings.[8] His methods do coincide with many of the interests of traditional economists. He directly addresses problems of income distribution; externalities; institutional structures such as modern corporations, monetary influences, public and private waste; the role of technology and growth; and much more. These are clearly elements of an economic model. The model, however, is a model of capitalism and not of a 'generic' economics. Heilbroner approaches all economic problems by not removing them from their social system. You cannot carve an economic piece out of modern society and evoke *ceteris paribus* for the rest. Understanding economics is the understanding of capitalism.

5 The Structure of Capitalism

Capitalism did not spring from some noble heritage or acute sense of self-purpose. Rather, it very slowly evolved, after the fall of Rome, from the initial pack trains of the burgher merchants. Heilbroner describes capitalism as emerging 'slowly, painfully, and without any sense of fulfilling a historic mission – during a thousand-year period we call feudalism' (Heilbroner 1993a, 50). The highly collective and strictly hierarchical social structure of Rome is, on the surface, incompatible with the capitalist system. Any belief in self-fulfillment and individual rights was still hundreds of years in the future. If capitalism had spontaneously risen to combat Roman intolerance it would be easier to relate to its success. In reality, capitalism was born after a thousand-year gestation; punctuated with disease, famine and human misery. Finding an appropriate method of viewing capitalism's character and heritage is a very difficult endeavour.

It is easy to fall under the economist's spell of imagining that individuals consistently strive to better their condition. As we saw in Chapter 2, neoclassical theory is based on the idea of marginal decisions being evaluated against a sounding-board of costs and benefits. Rational decisions are said to achieve consistency in the well-being of the economic agent. However, if we muster our courage and step out of the neoclassical's timeless bubble, history may tell us something quite different. I believe that few – economists included – would argue that life in the Dark Ages was more pleasant than life in Rome. Any measure of mankind's material well-being is never as straight and true as the trend line of a Real Business Cycle model. Technological progress is not the saviour that it is so often believed. The technologies of the Roman Empire were available to the inhabitants of the Dark Ages but they were somehow ignored. All technology is human centred in the sense that the members of a social system must *decide* to implement it. Moving from a society with the ability to transport food and grain from around the Mediterranean to Rome (a city of over one million people), with only the horse and cart,[1] to a social structure of independent feudal manors is difficult for the economist to explain. It does not fit the fundamental assumptions of traditional economic modelling.

Capitalism is more than an antiseptic collection of markets and price indicators. It is better described as a 'historical formation, distinguishable from formations that have preceded it, or that today parallel it, both by a core of central institutions and by the motion these institutions impart on the whole' (Heilbroner 1988b, 347). In other words, capitalism shares the same institutionalized human insecurities and petty schoolboy power struggles as ancient kingships or military dictatorships. The central difference is that capitalism's *raison d'être* is the drive to accumulate capital.

I will begin this chapter with a brief overview of Heilbroner's *nature* and *logic* of capitalism. We will see that his approach to understanding capitalism employs the human, social and economic elements of his methodology. It examines the internal dynamics of capitalism's social structure as well as the external properties of markets and business enterprise. From there we move to examining the three defining characteristics of capitalism. We will see that every capitalist system (in all their national flavours) contains the drive to accumulate capital, the existence of markets and the division of power between public and private realms. The chapter concludes with a brief look at the various ways economists view capitalism. It shows why the radical and conservative branches of economics disagree on the operation of, and policy prescriptions for, capitalism.

THE NATURE AND LOGIC OF THE REGIME OF CAPITALISM

Capitalism has taken a variety of shapes and forms over the years. Many speak of craft capitalism, industrial capitalism, corporate capitalism, and even modern capitalism. Each of these 'capitalisms' are attributed a variety of social benefits or cultural woes which separate them from other social entities. Over the years, the economic literature has absorbed the various 'capitalisms' with such ease that any true definition of a capitalist social system is often hard to find. It is even difficult to depict the 'economic' nature of the system. Heilbroner argues that:

> Capitalism cannot be adequately conceptualized as an 'economic system'. Rather, it must be understood as a regime. The term emphasizes that there must be an impelling force *behind* the business activities that are such a large part of capitalism, a force that cannot

be grasped or represented in the language of economics.

(Heilbroner 1988d, 65)

Capitalism is more than a market system or business civilization. It rests on a set of deeply internalized institutions and cultural values. Heilbroner chooses to describe capitalism in the broader terms of 'nature' and 'logic'. By shying away from the typical economic terminology, Heilbroner emphasizes the *regime* characteristic of the system. He defines the nature of the system as referring 'to its behavior-shaping institutions and relationships and the logic of capitalism as the pattern of configurational changes generated by this inner core' (Heilbroner 1985a, 19). Thus the nature of a system in turn gives rise to the historically unique logic.

The 'nature' of any social formation refers to the 'ensemble of elements that influence the behavior of its members, especially those kinds of behavior that drive the system along its particular historical path' (Heilbroner 1985a). Examples of this 'ensemble of elements' would include geography, climate and natural setting of the social formation. Humans react to their environment. They react within the bounds of the human species. This is why Heilbroner includes the human and social elements in his economics. He acknowledges that underlying any social formation is the continual interaction of human tendencies and the given (physical and social) environment. This interaction accounts for the evolution of behaviour-shaping institutions. Customs and mores of any society are the result of that society's shared cultural heritage. Therefore, understanding the 'nature' of a system is critical in projecting the 'logic' or trajectory of the system. If the cultural mores of a society dictate the distribution of its provisioning through explicit orders, such as the commands of a pharaoh or the laws of state, then that society would be considered to have a 'command' economy. Provisioning and distribution are achieved through coercion or threatened punishment. On the other hand, if the mores of a society dictate a more individual focus and the use of an allocating market mechanism, then the society operates with a 'market' economy. Each of the 'economic' formations are the result of the system's nature and logic. We will see that capitalism's drive to accumulate expresses much the same influence over the system as the drive for conquest does in a society based on imperial rule. It endows it with its own unique logic.

It is important to realize that the term logic in no way refers to any mathematical or Aristotelian logic. It is simply the consequence of the forces and institutions that give a society its nature. The term is used in a causal sense. Heilbroner writes:

> Thus the logic of a social formation refers to the movements of and changes in the 'life processes' and institutional configurations of a society. What is 'logical' about these movements is that they express the outcome of the system's nature, as a released spring expresses the energy stored up within it. Wherever there is social movement there is a matrix of shaping influences whence this movement issues.
> (Heilbroner 1985a, 25)

It is not my intention to give an extensive description of cultural formation or a detailed account of how institutions are formed. Something of that magnitude would fill the remains of this chapter and be of little use in our analysis of Heilbroner's economic vision. All that I wish to convey is that by expressing capitalism in terms of its inherent *nature* and *logic*, Heilbroner is able to present capitalism as a distinct social formation and place it in its proper historical setting. Further, he emphasizes the superficial nature of most economic inquiry. Any study that deals solely with market analysis may miss much of the capitalist system.

This is why Heilbroner's 'economics' contains the three elements of human, social and economic components. The surface veneer of business activity is only part of the capitalist order. The 'craft', or 'industrial', or 'corporate' epithet may accurately describe this changing veneer, but it does little to penetrate to the roots of the system. What is required is a set of defining characteristics which when taken collectively, offer a necessary and sufficient list of judgement criteria. Heilbroner lists these as: the drive to accumulate capital, the existence of markets, and the bifurcation of power into private (economic) and public (state) realms.

Capitalism, in all its historical formations, has contained each of these three elements. It also stands to reason, if capitalism is to be replaced with any alternate social structure, one or all of these must in turn be replaced. This is not to suggest that all capitalist systems are identical. This is certainly not the case. For example, capitalism in America is not the same as Japanese capitalism. The two differ greatly in the degree of separation of power and cooperation between the public and private realms. The roots of this difference lie in the underlying cultural variations of each country and not in the fundamental economic nature of capitalism. To understand the basic character of capitalism, it is useful to explore each of the defining characteristics in greater detail.

THE DRIVE TO ACCUMULATE CAPITAL

The drive to accumulate capital lies at the heart of all capitalist systems. I must stress from the outset that capital is not simply a surplus. Many ancient societies had the ability to generate a large surplus but they were not capitalisms. Ancient Egypt or Rome was capable of amassing a much larger surplus than was required for maintaining the empire. Their surplus was applied to religious or public monuments, military works or luxury consumption (Heilbroner 1988b, 347) but not to the accumulation of capital.

Further, wealth is not capital. Heilbroner writes that Julius Caesar returned from his governorship of Spain a wealthy man but not a capitalist (Heilbroner 1993a, 49). Also, wealth is not an object of virtue. It is more a symbol of power and prestige, a convenient scorecard. Wealth measures and grants power to the one who owns it. This is not to suggest that there is no linkage between wealth and capitalism. There clearly is a link. It simply means that wealth is not a defining characteristic as wealth is present in many other social orders.

Heilbroner describes wealth as 'the economic face of political strat-ification, lodged in the hands of a class whose ability to grant or deny access to resources becomes the "economic" basis for both prestige and power' (Heilbroner 1988c, 882). It would be easy to argue that capital serves the same purpose. The motivations look the same on the surface but we must realize that a capitalist may strive to gain wealth, but he does it *through* capital acquisition. A capitalist can become wealthy 'on coal or scrap metal, which no one could imagine as wealth' (Heilbroner 1993a, 46). The capitalist does not wish to accumulate capital for the sake of the physical attributes of that capital. The capitalist accumulates capital only to be used in a circuit of production – sale for money– and further production. More correctly, Heilbroner states: *'capital is not a material thing but rather a process that uses material things as moments in its continuously dynamic existence'* [italics in original] (Heilbroner 1985a, 36–7). This process is best described in Marx's schema of M–C–M'. This circuit describes the process where money capital (M) is exchanged for commodities (C), to be sold for a larger money sum (M').

The commodities produced and technological attributes of production vary widely from economy to economy. However, the M–C–M' circuit is consistent within all capitalist systems. The circuit exemplifies the continually expansive nature of capitalism. Money capital can never sit idle. It must always be turned over in the M–C–M' circuit. One capitalist is always in danger of falling victim to another. Each capitalist must seek to win back his extended capital through increases in market share or the introduction of new commodities. Competition is bred from the capitalist's drive to accumulate rather than from having a large number of firms in any given market.

This competition and emphasis on economic expansion leads to extensive 'commodification'. The drive to accumulate causes business to bring activities, which were normally within the domain of private households, into the accumulation circuit. Economic growth is achieved simply by moving an activity into a sector where it is counted in the GDP figures. Activities such as recreation, cooking, cleaning and laundry are now provided as a service from private business. Hence, these are turned into commodities. This commodification has a profound influence in creating new lifestyles and social situations. Social structure is transformed through this continual drive to offer new products.

These new products are not limited to end-use consumer goods and services. Perhaps the most dynamic result of capital circulation is the development of new technologies and production processes. When this technological innovation lowers the costs of production, the capitalist enjoys an advantage analogous to that of a fortunately situated, low-cost landlord (Heilbroner 1985a, 73). These Schumpeterian rents[2] can take the form of capital improvements or simple changes in production management. Increases in labour quality or efficiency can have the same impact on cost reduction as any deepening of the capital stock. The important thing to remember, however, is the increase in profits caused by this cost reduction belongs to the capitalist and not the labour input. Capitalism's extensive legal system of property rights gives ownership of these 'residuals' to the capitalist. We do not need to delve into a detailed examination of Marxist class structure to see that the M–C–M' circuit is heavily weighted in favour of the owners of the means of production. Workers are paid money wages by the capitalist and any surplus or profit the worker produces is automatically (structurally) returned to the capitalist. Workers do have the ability to bargain for higher wages. However, by design they cannot be equal to the profit they produce. Their employing firm[3] must be able to 'stay in business'.

Acknowledging the M–C–M' process does not explain the underlying human desire to amass wealth. Most economists would argue that behind the desire to amass wealth is the desire to increase 'utility' or the 'desire of bettering our condition'. Heilbroner, on the other hand, suggests:

> The unappeasable character of the expansive drive for capital suggests, however, that its roots lie not so much in these conscious motivations as in the gratification of unconscious drives, specifically the universal infantile need for affect and experience of frustrated aggression. Such needs and drives surface in all societies as the desires for prestige and for personal domination. From this point of view, capitalism appears not as an 'economic system' knit by the appeals of mutually advantageous exchange, but as a larger cultural setting in which the pursuit of wealth fulfils the same unconscious purpose as did the pursuit of military glory or celebration of personal majesty in earlier epochs.   (Heilbroner 1988b, 348)

This explanation of the acquisitive nature of humans fits much neater into human history. If capitalism should be regarded as a regime as Heilbroner suggests, then it must be clearly explained within a historical context. Capitalism must be shown to have evolved from, and share common elements with, previous social formations.

The roots of the capitalist order extend into the ruins of the fallen Roman Empire. Heilbroner explains:

> Beginning as early as the tenth century, the mercantile estate found the protective shelter it needed in the rubble of the fiefdoms that emerged from that enormous collapse. Very gradually, there arose from the widening importance of mercantile dealings, and from the increasing dependence of all levels of society on the market mechanism, the foundations of the regime of capital itself.

(Heilbroner 1985a, 87)

Merchant traders, who had established trading niches in the ninth and tenth centuries, began to organize production in the towns. The feudal lord continued to oversee production by the peasants on the manors and estates. By the twelfth and thirteenth centuries, the merchant class (and the descending guild master) began to gain considerable political influence. The transformation of the 'merchant estate' into an independent capitalist class took centuries to complete. According to

Heilbroner it was not 'legitimated until the English revolution of the 17th and the French revolution of the 18th centuries' (Heilbroner 1988b, 348). However, by the end of the nineteenth century the 'burgher' class had transformed itself into the powerful bourgeois. With the rise of the bourgeois came the advent of a money-minded mind set. Drive for personal gain was socially legitimized. Social relationships were directed by the interaction of master and apprentice, buyer and seller. This transformation was augmented by the 'gradual remonetization of medieval European life that accompanied its political reconstitution' (Heilbroner 1988b, 348). The replacement of feudal relationships with market-oriented ones caused power to drift from the aristocrat to the merchant. Wealth accompanied power and by the end of the nineteenth century, the merchant bourgeois class was firmly entrenched and the market was a way of life.

MARKETS AND CAPITALISM

The market is by far the most often cited characteristic of capitalism. However this institution, which has been endowed with an almost divine power by the conservative press, is less important to our study than its flanking brethren. The market exerts a binding force on the system as a whole but it is not the source of capitalist energy. That, of course, is the drive for capital. The market or more precisely, a web of markets, does however bind the individual interests of the participating buyers and sellers. It also acts as a personal shield for the participants. A 'down' market or bad market 'conditions' is ample justification for massive layoffs or fiscal cutbacks. Such behaviour would be frowned upon (and openly condemned) if it originated within the human soul of the business owner. But since it is the result of the 'impersonal' market, almost any behaviour is accepted without question. This then raises a very interesting and almost *koan* sounding question. Can markets exist without their human participants? I pose this question only half in jest.

In today's world of supermarkets, stock markets and even flea markets, one begins to wonder just how far removed the market participants are from the true meaning of the word. How much has the institution of 'the market' permeated into the cultural bedrock? Has the behaviour-shaping influence of accepted market activity actually changed the participant's definition of the institution? These are interesting questions that beg clarification.

Heilbroner describes markets as 'the conduits through which the energies of the system flow and the mechanism by which the private realm can organize its tasks without the direct intervention of the public realm' (Heilbroner 1993a, 96). In other words, in a market society the means of production and distribution are orchestrated through the vast exchange between sellers and buyers. This differs from the term market used to describe ancient or feudal societies. These societies had 'markets' – places for exchange – but they did not organize the fundamental provisioning activities of the society. The 'prices' in these markets were set exogenously from the free exchange of buyers and sellers. The rise of the market system had to wait until the necessary ideologies (Appleby 1978) were in place. In a society without the drive to accumulate, markets were products of geography not psychology. In markets without a 'maximizing mind set', markets fail to function. This is what links it with capitalism.

The market rests on several fundamental assumptions of human nature. If any of these are removed the coordinating nature of the market would cease to function. The first assumption is that individuals follow whatever path best promotes their economic self-interest. This means they consistently seek the highest paying jobs and always seek to lower their expenditure. This means they will freely move into whatever occupation or geographic region that will pay them the most. Business owners would do the same. They would gladly shift their capital to various industries and locations. All this says is that labour and capital are mobile. They are free to move toward incentives provided by the market.

The second assumption is a little more complex. It addresses the relationships and conflicts the system produces on the same side (that is, buyer versus buyer and seller versus seller) of the market. For example, in the labour market the workers compete against each other in an effort to secure the highest paying job. Sellers also compete among themselves for limited market share. This means that all market competition is not only 'cross-market' or buyer versus seller. Heilbroner writes:

> The market system thereby becomes its own policing agency against the exactions of greed and the inequalities of exploitation. Oddly enough, this self-policing process is also driven to by self-interest, even when this involves reducing one's immediate gain. The supplier who will not lower a price is out of line and will be bypassed in favor

of another; a buyer who will not meet the going market price will not
be able to purchase what his competitor can.

(Heilbroner 1993a, 100)

Each of these assumptions are directed at establishing what Adolph
Lowe has called sufficient 'micro-order'. Any social system must display sufficient order if its distribution system is to operate. This raises
the question of how order might be obtained in non-market societies.
If we take command-planned economies as an example, we see that
inventories could provide this mechanism. If planners were to watch
inventory levels as closely as marketeers watch prices, they would get
the same information. The inventory level would act as a signal, much
the same as a price signal. Producers would increase production as
inventories fell and, conversely, would reduce output if they rose. The
production process would work much the same as it does in a market
economy. The enemy of such a system is any bureaucratic blockages.
The process also assumes the planner has the necessary power to
actually control the process. The real difficulty comes in the form of
bureaucratic lags in the direction of timing the production. This is
what led Oscar Lange to write: ' The real danger of socialism is that
of a bureaucratization of economic life' (Lange and Taylor 1938).
Heilbroner appends this with the comment:

What Lange should have said was something else: the great source of
disorder in command economies is the absence of a framework in
which self-interest leads to socially useful action.

(Heilbroner 1993a, 102)

It is the lack of any human motivational structure that leads to failure
of command-planned systems; social systems are by definition human-
oriented. In reality, inventory levels work the same as prices because in
the day-to-day production of the market system, it is the level of a
firm's inventory that actually motivates production. In an age of
administered prices and contractual delivery commitments, inventory
levels are the proxy for price. True market prices are a very rare
commodity. In most cases it is the *level* of prices which supply the
signal. Firms see an approximate average of prices in their market, not
an individual price point.

Before we conclude our look at capitalist markets it is important
that we touch on the inherent fragility of the system. I will cover this in
greater detail when we direct our gaze toward the future in Chapter

five, but, for now, we should realize markets may not support the system forever. In this I am not referring to market failures such as public goods or externalities. What I wish to address is the fragility that is amplified as the system becomes more complex. As capitalist systems mature, and capital equipment develops a more specialized purpose, the production process becomes more 'fixed'. This more 'fixed' nature of the system reduces the system's mobility. As the mobility is reduced (a violation of our first assumption), the resulting rigidity adds a certain fragility. Heilbroner provides the simile:

> Capitalist societies start as sandpile and end up as girded structures...A pile of sand will hold its shape against many blows, but a structure of girders, although incomparably larger and stronger than the sand pile, can topple by the collapse of a single, strategically placed beam.   (Heilbroner 1993a, 104)

The moral of this story is clear: as capitalist systems become more complex and industries are built on the implied behaviour (and existence) of linked cooperation, the strength of the system resides in its weakest link. The most efficient production facilities rely on the transportation sector and the most sophisticated computer facility is dependent on its electronic power supplier. The system is a complex web of implied relationships. Capitalism is less a system of smokestacks and ornate boardrooms than it is of handshakes in ordinary back rooms.

PUBLIC AND PRIVATE POWER

The varying gradients of the separation of power between the public and private realms is what gives competing capitalisms their distinct character. If we compare American capitalism to Japanese or Swedish we find that it is not the drive to accumulate or the existence of markets that provides the differences. It is the degree of separation between the state and private realms that actually defines each system. In fact, the separation of power not only provides us with a spectrum of capitalisms, but it defines the overall nature of the social structure. In no other historical order is the division of power so compartmentalized. It traditionally fell to the state to provide both the production and provisioning as well as the more typical political tasks like the enforcement of law or the conduct of war. It is only in capitalism that this is divided. The idea of leaving the material provisioning to self-motivated farmers and merchants would never have been considered by Aristotle or Machiavelli (Heilbroner 1993a, 69). Economic activities were sufficiently routine or traditionalized that the state did not have to meddle. The unabridged power of the state removed any 'economy' from earlier societies.

Heilbroner's reluctance to grant precaptitalist societies an economy is something unique. He writes:

> ...there was no economy in precapitalist societies for the same reason that there was no economics. To be sure, all the necessary activities of production and distribution were in evidence, but they were in no way subject to a different social discipline from their larger social and political functions.   (Heilbroner 1993a, 70)

The 'economy' was so intertwined with the political hierarchy that any separate inquiry was not needed. Before the drive for capital bestowed the economic motion, the logic of the system was explained through the political structure. It was only after the installation of separate economic motivations that the need for any 'economics' would arise. This is why Heilbroner's 'worldly philosophers' were all from an era of capitalist social systems. It is also the reason why his economics is based on capitalism. Without an economic realm, there is not economics.

The proper dividing line between the public and private realms is as heavily contested as the 38th parallel. Political parties and philosophical ideologies divine their very existence from this controversial issue. Fortunately, in our inquiry, we need not address the proper mix but only recognize the historical uniqueness of the division. Capitalism's severing of the 'seamless web of rulership' (Heilbroner 1988b, 349) has several important ramifications.

The first is the degree of tension between the realms. The economic realm provides the momentum to the system. We have seen that the drive for capital that is channelled through markets, is what provides for capitalism's growth. The government side of capitalism is to provide the supervision and protection of the system. Military might and legal infrastructure remove the majority of threats which may keep the capitalist from venturing his capital. The dividing line is very imprecisely drawn and the public and private realms rely heavily on each other for support. The two have formed an alliance which is indispensable for the maintenance of the system. For example, it falls to the government to provide the 'non-economic' infrastructure. Heilbroner explains:

Government, not the economy, is responsible for the well-being of the work force; for its adequate training and education, for the law and order that undergird all contractual relationships, for the provision of public goods without which the private sector could not operate, not to mention such directly economic measures as the creation and regulation of a money supply. Without these, the private realm could not last more than momentarily.

(Heilbroner 1988d, 67)

This tacit interconnection between public and private realms makes classifying capitalism a 'private' enterprise system a profound mistake. The system is anything but a private system. Conservative business may call for laissez-faire policy but they could not survive without the public support structure. In American capitalism the interconnection may not be as noticeable as in the European Airbus cooperation, but it is nonetheless real. American politics and enterprise are very closely tied.

Any comparison of two so closely tied powers leads one to speculate on which is the strongest. On the surface, most would argue that it is the state. After all, they control the military complex and the legal system. At any point in time they could hypothetically stop a facility from producing. However, if we expand our time horizon, the economic side may have an edge. No state could survive without sufficient goods and services that sustain a country.

We cannot see the true power of capital until we take a global view. The power of any given nation-state is severely limited when we see the truly international character of capital. In a world of international markets, international corporations and global financial markets, capital is becoming more independent. As capital becomes more international, the individual nation-states become less able to control production. Stringent environmental regulations in one country result in the production being relocated to another. In the pursuit of profit, capital finds the least cost environment.

Traditional economic literature is full of such power comparisons. Its journals are full of the pros and cons of international trade laws and global policy prescriptions. I have to stress that it is not possible to make any such power comparisons (beyond a very short time span) because of the endemic interconnections between capital and the state. Neither capital nor the state could survive without the other within a capitalist system. The state could, of course, overtake and 'nationalize' the production but at that point we no longer have capitalism. We have

moved into a socialist framework. Without the division of power we no
longer have capitalism.

We have seen that the three defining characteristics of capitalism are
the drive to accumulate capital, the existence of the market and the
separation of the power between the public and private realms.
Remove any of these and capitalism as a social entity cannot survive.
The drive to accumulate which is conducted through markets is essentially the same in all capitalisms. It falls to the separation of power to
give a capitalism its national character. This dividing line is often
argued and with little result. It is not where the line is drawn but the
existence of the line that is important as a definitional tool. This is not
to say that it is unimportant where the line is drawn. Where the line is
drawn will no doubt delineate the economic winners and losers. Heilbroner believes the placement of the line is critical. He states:

> In my opinion no single issue will be more profoundly determinative
> of the future of the system than the relation between the two realms.
> I do not mean there exists some 'optimal' mix of public and private
> spheres. On the contrary, I am certain that the configuration will
> vary from country to country, depending on many elements, not
> least that of 'national character'.   (Heilbroner 1993a, 90)

This problem of the proper mix of the public and private spheres is
often what separates various schools of economic thought. Most often
it is the conservative schools that are seen to wish less public intervention and the radical who want more government activity. While the
separation between schools is more of a methodological or ideological
focus, it is worth a few moments to explore the popularly perceived
differences. After all, if we cannot agree on what capitalism is, it is very
difficult to project its future. This look should also provide a very
concrete example of Heilbroner's economic vision. With the core of
his 'economics' being deeply rooted in an understanding of capitalism,
it is imperative we understand how he differentiates the various views
on the system.

CONSERVATIVE AND RADICAL ECONOMICS ON
CAPITALISM

Just as conservative and radical political parties fail to agree on the
proper role of government, conservative and radical economists fail to

agree on a mutual definition of capitalism. Heilbroner argues that this disagreement on the fundamentals of the capitalist system is due to political frictions. He states: 'economists disagree because they are political animals, and because the practice of economics, like any social analysis, is shot through with political suppositions and assumptions of its protagonists' (Heilbroner 1984, 2). In 'Capitalism as *Gestalt*: A Contrast of Visions', Heilbroner sets forth a listing of conservative and radical tenets. He lists five theses that to his mind, capture the modern conservative position and seven which define the radical. I will set down each of the listings before we attempt any comparison or analysis.

Conservative

(1) Capitalism is a 'natural' economic system. Conservatives believe that capitalism is in alliance with human nature and mankind will spontaneously drift toward capitalism once any social impediments are removed.
(2) Capitalism is an evolutionary system.
(3) Growth arises naturally within capitalism from the interplay of its two elemental constituents. The first of these constituents is the profit motive and the second is the restraining mechanism of competition.
(4) The capitalist economy contains two sectors, one public and the other private. The private sector is responsible for growth and the public sector is responsible for defence, law and order and the production of public goods.
(5) Capitalism is an international system in that the nation-states are bound together by market forces. The world economy therefore exerts a restraining and ultimately a commanding force over the movements of its national capitalist members.

Radical

(1) Capitalism is quintessentially a means of organizing labour to produce a social surplus.
(2) Capitalism is not the first surplus-producing system. Other civilizations such as ancient Egypt or European feudalism generated surplus. However, in capitalism surplus is employed to create the means to gather additional surplus. In other words, wealth in capitalism takes the form of machines, plant and equipment.

(3) Surplus under capitalism accumulates as a consequence of the existence of wage labour as the mode by which production is carried on. Further, the wage-labour system is historically unique in that it legally denies the worker ownership of his labour-product.

(4) The separation of work from the right to claim the product of work establishes the rational for the organization of the work process that is typical of capitalism. The 'division of labour' is not a natural tendency of mankind and it is not found in other societies to the degree that it exists in capitalism.

(5) The productive activities of capitalism are coordinated by market exchange among individuals and firms.

(6) The wage-labour system effectively creates an 'economy' distinct from society. This bifurcation causes several types of problems to occur. First is the consequence of excluding social consequence from economic decisions. The rise of the factory creates 'mill' towns; the breakdown of the extended family is caused by wage-labour relations. The second problem is the continuing difficulty in absorbing the successfully generated surplus. The radical view stresses the self-generated quality of each of these problems.

(7) Capitalism is a world system, but not merely because it is linked by market forces. The core of the system is the extension of the wage-labour system from the developed centre to the unde-veloped periphery.

Heilbroner admits that this is not far from being a complete listing. However, it does provide enough to contrast the two economic approaches. It is obvious from the list that even though there are a few overlaps, they are essentially two different *gestalts*. The two camps view capitalism as two very different systems and therefore have two different research paradigms and sets of policy prescriptions. In Heilbroner's view 'the essential difference between them is the absence of a historic dimension in the conservative view' (Heilbroner 1984, 6).

This lack of historic perspective helps explain the preoccupation with 'equilibrium' that is displayed by neoclassical theory. If the system has a tendency to rest in some natural equilibrium state then the idea of movement through historical time is not a paramount concern. Couple this with the belief that capitalism occurs 'naturally' and you get an idea of why the conservative theory has developed as it has. The conservative view that in the absence of any artificial impediment and distortions by the government, the economy will reach equilibrium and harmony is completely in line with the mathematical precision they have striven for in conservative theory. Economic behaviour is best approximated with well-behaved mathematical functions. Economic growth may move around the trend but those movements are short-lived and of limited severity. Essentially, there are not economic or social contradictions in the system.

The radical economic camp takes a nearly opposite view. To them the system tends toward disequilibrium and crisis. The continuous tensions between the class systems and the inability of the capitalist to gauge the rate at which surplus can be absorbed by the system actually give capitalism its dynamic nature. Radicals see the entire process working against the idea of harmony. This, of course, is why Marx chose the dialectical methodology.

Another glaring difference is in the related area of economic waste. For conservative economists, there is no economic waste in the production of anything that sells. Conservatives are quick to point to government waste in all forms. They quickly condemn bureaucratic squandering or redundancies while never applying similar criteria to the private sector. If something sells it provides jobs and income. Radicals take a nearly opposite view. Something is waste if it fulfills no useful purpose. Trivial goods or trivial differentiation of goods is wasteful in a society where there are so many in need of the basics of life.

Just as the definition of waste differs, the role of government is entirely different in the two visions. The conservative side sees government as an intruder or blockage to the economic process. They see government as creating distortions and artificial impediments in the 'naturally' occurring capitalism. To the conservative, equilibrium cannot be achieved if government is not carefully directed away from the system. The radical view of the proper role of government is not as clear. For the radical, the designation of private and public refers to functions of the capitalist order. Both public and private functions are seen as supporting the process of surplus generation. But one thing is clear in the radical view: the governing element is responsible for curbing the activities of the privileged groups within the system. The success of the capitalist private sector can actually harm the inhabitants if left unrestrained. The profit motive that drives wages below subsistence, shifting of externalities to the non-producing public, or the widening nature of income distribution all need to be addressed if the society can continue to function without social failure.

Where does Heilbroner fit into all this? In his own words:

> ... it must be apparent that my own *gestalt* lies much closer to the radical than the conservative view. I should perhaps add that there are elements in the older conservative tradition, exemplified in Smith's *Theory of Moral Sentiments*, that seem to me to fill large lacunae in the radical analysis – elements that deal with the nature of authority and hierarchy ...   (Heilbroner 1984, 9–10)

Not wishing to simply say that his own view resides more in the radical *gestalt* he adds: 'The policies and programs of the modern conservative economics have, to my mind, brought great and unnecessary hardship to the Western world, and my basic intent is to plumb the conceptions on which these policies and programs ultimately rest' (Heilbroner 1984, 10).

This brief quotation goes a long way in explaining his reluctance to concentrate on economic policy. As we saw in Chapter 1, Heilbroner has never taken a substantial stance in this arena. This reluctance to forming policy is directly related to his dissatisfaction with conservative economic theory. If a policy is to be remotely considered, it must fit loosely in the mostly conservative current environment. Any policy formation also implicitly assumes that the underlying economic process is functioning consistently. This may not be the case. If an economy is unable to generate any macro-order[4] then no typical policy is of use. This, of course, assumes that the policy is not an attempt to generate this macro order.

Heilbroner's willingness to predict future events may be related to Lowe's instrumental method.[5] In this method Lowe takes a carefully generated view of a future economic state as given and the motivations needed to achieve as the unknown. This is not consistent with the dominant methodology in economics. The *hypothetico-deductive* approach requires that general laws of human behaviour are formed and then the future is logically deduced from these laws. Lowe believed that the order-bestowing behaviours such as maximization had lost much of their ability to create sufficient level or order. The time horizons in production and consumption and the expectation decision process have been extended to the point that it was rational to not maximize.[6] For Lowe, it falls to policy makers to enact policy which would restore these motivations. Policy should not focus exclusively on changing variables such as money supply to reach a desired level of investment. This type of policy formation assumes we know how the economic agents will react. Without sufficient order, nobody knows how the agents will react. The initial laws of the hypothetico-deductive approach may be incorrect. If this is the case, government intervention is a matter of chance. Lowe's instrumental-deductive method concentrates on generating the '*suitable conditions for goal attainment*' (Lowe 1969). In a nutshell, the 'knowns' are the initial state of the economy, a macro-goal (the future state) and certain laws or rules which help us understand how the economic agents will react. The unknowns are the actual path the economy will take, the actual individual patterns the agents will display, and the presence of any external influences which may arise during the process.

It is clear that in this method the most important 'known' is the destination of the system. Therefore, a good projection of the trajectory of the capitalist system is imperative. This type of forecasting is well beyond the scope of econocentric technicians. The future social conditions as well as the future economic conditions must be projected. These future conditions must then be weighed together to see how the interaction of the public and private faces of capitalism react. The process is less an exercise in deduction than it is an application of social analysis. Heilbroner's economic method is invaluable to the process as we will see in our next chapter 'A View To the Future'.

6 A View to the Future

Any discussion of capitalism's future rapidly evokes deeply rooted and often polarized views. Capitalism embodies what is right or what is wrong with the world. For some, a future of capitalism stands for liberty and happiness, for others repression and despair. Many are quick to predict specific changes in capitalism's nature. Some envision a future of computers and robotics, home offices and telecommuting, multinational corporations and global market places. Why does this social conjuring hold such a fascination for so many? The answer is simple: for millions of people around the globe, consciously or unconsciously, capitalism is their life.

Heilbroner has long been credited with providing us economic 'visions' of our future. From *The Worldly Philosophers* in 1953 to *The Crisis of Vision* in 1996, he has laboured to provide a social framework that may help us decipher our future. His own ideas have evolved over the years but his method has remained the same. He does not bother with specific forecasts such as GDP levels on the year 2050. As Heilbroner said in 1972, 'I am not interested in the minutia of economics' (Heilbroner 1972). The predictions display the same characteristics as his economics; they are sweeping, penetrating and human-centred.

This chapter will begin with a look at his method of viewing the economic future. We will see that he cultivates what he calls a 'future related understanding'. This understanding is a model which describes how the capitalist system unfolds. It is not specific to a single nation-state, but rather can be used to understand capitalism in all its forms. From there we move to Heilbroner's specific outlook for capitalism. We see the internal dynamics of the system give it a tremendous resiliency and properties of self-reinforcement. The division of power provides the institutional support and the drive to accumulate supplies the regenerating logic.

A FUTURE RELATED UNDERSTANDING

Heilbroner first coins the expression 'future related understanding' in his 1993 book *21st Century Capitalism*. The term is new but the heart of the analysis is not. It continues the thread which runs through all

Heilbroner's work, namely understanding the sociopolitical nature of economics. Future related understanding is nothing more than seeing capitalism as a social system, the future trajectory of which is dependent on its internal metabolism of the drive to accumulate. By focusing on this internal drive, Heilbroner's model is applicable to all capitalist systems. Heilbroner explains:

> Looking at capitalism from this unaccustomed perspective puts into our hands a way of thinking about the future that we would not have if we approached the problem from the viewpoint of one country, even one that we know very well. The difference is that we become aware of capitalism as a system with a basic orientation discoverable in all its individual national embodiments.
>
> (Heilbroner 1993a, 21)

Approaching the future of capitalism as an understanding of the system in total, with all the institutional and political elements intact, Heilbroner shows us a future that is a logical extension of the past. This is best described by his 1959 book title, *The Future as History*. Capitalism is not a static system. It is a continual interaction of capital and technology, public and private powers, and new and old institutional restraints. The trajectory of the system is a direct result of previous long-term change. Just as capitalism required a thousand-year gestation, any critical change in its operation will likely be the result of a previous socialized change. I am certainly not arguing that there will be no external 'shocks' which disrupt production. There will, of course, always be shocks like oil embargos or natural disasters. These will always result in production anomalies or perhaps even be the catalyst for transformational changes. Capitalism's trajectory is the result of the systemic energy it internally generates, releasing its energy like a coiled spring.

Following Heilbroner's lead of seeing the future as history, it may be useful to return to his past to see how he views his present. As confusing as that sounds, in 1974 Heilbroner wrote an article (Heilbroner 1974b) which examined the problems of the day (stagflation, environmental restraints, etc.) as resulting from their historical inertia. He speaks to that day's current problems as he might have seen them in the 1950s. While the article does not list any policy prescriptions, it does explain why the economics profession failed to see the problems coming. It failed because the traditional economic model views only the surface of capitalism. If hindsight is 20/20 and retrospect is circumspect, then this approach may prove beneficial. It gives us a glimpse of Heilbroner's model in action with its author in the announcer's booth.

THE CLOUDED CRYSTAL BALL

Heilbroner begins by taking a very wide view of the day's economic problems. He lists growth and inflation, the constraint of the environment,[1] Japan's re-entry into the world market, the rise of the multinational, economic development, and the deficiency of traditional economic policy. He opens by stating:

> Three aspects are common to all these 'future' problems of the past. First, they are all economic, rather than political and sociological. Second, they are all deep-seated rather than 'accidental' or superficial economic problems. Last, and most important, *everyone of these problems was invisible in the 1950s*.   (Heilbroner 1974b, 121)

Classifying each as 'economic' emphasizes his view that they are all systemic of capitalist 'economies'. They are economic in that in any econocentric society, most disruptions are viewed as economic problems. These problems leave economic footprints. Second, labelling the problems as 'deep-seated' reinforces the socioeconomic interdependence of the capitalist structure. 'Deep-seated' references a strata of interconnections which lie below the surface of the business economy. Third, the invisibility of the problems, emphasizes the fact that none would have been forecast through traditional econometric efforts. Time-series analysis or today's co-integration models can only track pre-existing or 'previously-surfaced' problems; they track the scores of games already played. Games yet to be played are the domain of the clairvoyant and the gambler.

In the article, Heilbroner could not have made these more modern econometric extensions. Heilbroner writes:

> Before I attempt to peer into the clouded crystal ball, let me ruminate on why the great body of economists failed to predict the major trends of economic affairs over the past two decades. I can suggest four reasons for this failure: perhaps there are others. First, the perceptual capabilities of the human mind make it genuinely difficult to perceive new 'problems' in any field. Events bombard us in seemingly random fashion ... we rarely discern a problem that is

'latent,' although after the fact it is all too easy to discover its premonitory warnings. The second... we tend to organize our perceptions according to received doctrines which are well understood – and find it difficult to formulate new paradigms that will reorder data according to a different set of rules... Third, it is difficult to formulate cogent long-term trends because the indeterminacy of the economic system is greater than in the past. The policy issues of the 1970's will not emerge solely as the outcome of blind market forces, but will be 'made' in Washington, Tokyo, Paris, Bonn... Fourth and last, predictions are difficult because there exist connections between economic trends and sociological or political behavior patterns about which we know very little.   (Heilbroner 1974b, 122)

These explanations of why economists have failed to predict should look familiar. With the exception of the first, they are the same reasons Heilbroner will list as possible causes for the failure of worldly philosophy (see Chapter 3). Heilbroner includes them in this 1974 article but they will surface in the 6th edition (1986) of *The Worldly Philosophers* and again in 'Is a Worldly Philosophy Still Possible' (1992).

In 'The Clouded Crystal Ball' Heilbroner credits the major problems of the 1970s to a 'severe dysfunction or even nonfunction of parts of the economic system rather than with the main macro-aggregate' (Heilbroner 1974b, 122). In other words, changes in the macro-aggregates, which are the main focus of traditional economics, may be lagging indicators of economic change. Traditional theory virtually ignores the sociopolitical nature of economics. Heilbroner believes any policy built on the behavioural assumptions of neoclassical theory will have difficulty because they 'are too far from reality to produce models in which we can place much confidence' (Heilbroner 1974b, 123). The theory actually veils our understanding of the system. In this case what the theory veiled is the breakdown of micro-order. The institutional substructure of the system has changed from the late 1950s. Changes in bankruptcy laws, fiscal policy stabilizers and a bureaucratization of public and private organizations allow the typical reaction times to lengthen. Shocks which hit the system may not surface as quickly or in the same way as theory expected. Therefore, the breakdown of the 'forecasts' were really failures of underlying theory.

I have detoured into the past to emphasize this point: failures in economic prediction are the result of shortcomings in the underlying economic model. In the 1974 article Heilbroner is not able to elegantly pinpoint the exact watershed which caused the problems of stagflation or environmental restraints. What he is able to do is emphasize the limitations of an 'economic' theory that confines itself to surface price movements. He is calling for a theory which sees the capitalist system as a regime that is driven by the accumulation of capital. This makes his 'future related understanding' analogous to his general hermeneutic methodology. When Heilbroner presents visions of the future they are in fact 'scenarios' in the worldly philosophy tradition. The work of Marx, Smith and Schumpeter may have failed to anticipate all of capitalism's twists and turns, but they did embody a framework for viewing the future.

THE DISTANT PAST, YESTERDAY, TODAY

Heilbroner also gives us a framework for viewing the future. In his book *Visions of the Future* (1995) he separates human history into three broad epochs and traces economic development through each. The Distant Past, Yesterday and Today represents those periods of time, each with its own unique properties of provisioning. Each provisioning method also influenced how that society viewed its future. The key question is: How much control did each have in governing their own destiny?

The Distant Past refers to all of 'human existence from the appearance of Homo sapiens 150,000 years ago down to Yesterday, which begins a mere two or three hundred years ago' (Heilbroner 1995, 6). The social organizations of the Distant Past include primitive society, the kingdoms and empires of Rome and Mesopotamia, and finally the modern nation-state of Europe in the seventeenth century. What unifies this huge block of history is a sense of changelessness that surrounded the material provisioning of the society. Heilbroner explains:

> ... dynastic dreams were dreamt and visions of triumph or ruin were entertained; but there is no mention in the papyri and cuneiform tablets on which these hopes and fears were recorded that they envisaged, in the slightest degree, changes in the material conditions of the great masses of the people, or for that matter, of the ruling class itself.
> (Heilbroner 1995, 8)

The material side of life was conducted according to custom and traditional ways. With very few exceptions, the technologies and tools of production were the same from generation to generation.

There was no exclusive economic focus of any real significance. Capitalism had yet to take control of the lives of the people. The true capitalist class would not be in place until the seventeen hundreds. Religion served as the sense of hope in the Distant Past. It spoke of a promising afterlife but it also warned against violating codes of behaviour. Codes like the Ten Commandments were to be obeyed as they had always been. This supported the changelessness of the times. Any changes in the future were seen to be outside the control of the majority of the people. They tended to rely on the king or pharaohs or mythical gods for direction. There was not any true sense of self-generated change.

The period Heilbroner calls Yesterday is 'more accurately described as the rise and flourishing of capitalism, with its sister forces of technology and science and of an emerging political consciousness' (Heilbroner 1995,10). It is in this period (the beginning of the eighteenth century to the middle of the twentieth) that mankind began to realize it could shape its own future. This created a new sense of confidence in the future. The drive to accumulate capital endowed a general motion to the system. The technological and scientific improvements, which surfaced as a response to the accumulation, could be seen to control, or at least survive, the forces of nature. Life was no longer a reaction to exogenous events.

The rise of capitalism was not fast or evenly distributed. Therefore, this new confidence in the future was not evenly distributed. It resided only in industrialized capitalist countries. Africa, Latin America, and parts of Asia continued with the outlook of the Distant Past. This makes the period Yesterday, a combination of Yesterday and the Distant Past. He explains:

> Yesterday therefore remained, for almost all its two and a half centuries, an amalgam of two periods, in which the inertia of the Distant Past continued to form the expectations of the greater bulk of humanity, while the conditions of a new era lifted the hopes of those who lived in that handful of nations for whom the decisive page in history's book had been turned.   (Heilbroner 1995, 12–13)

This division of hope is consistent with the development of world capitalist systems. The capital formation resides in the developed centre and spreads outward to the periphery as production is moved to lower-cost alternatives. Profits are then channelled back to the developed centre.

The period Today began sometime between the end of the Second World War and the collapse of the Soviet Union. It started at a time of industrial capitalism and maturing political formations. Industrialized society had time to sufficiently incorporate the institutional base of capitalism into its general culture and the political realm had softened the more inhumane properties of the system. This softening would include child labour laws, unemployment insurance and welfare programs. This more thorough grounding of capitalism within modern society has had a dramatic influence on how we face the future. The continual advancement of science and technology creates large changes in daily life in how we view our daily lives. According to Heilbroner:

> ... if there was ever a time in which the shape of things to come was seen as dominated by impersonal forces, it is ours. Science, economics, mass political movements – the three most powerful carriers of those future-shaping influences – are the stuff of everyday headlines. What differentiates them from Yesterday is that they now appear as potentially or even actively malign as well as benign; both as threatening and supportive...
>
> (Heilbroner 1995, 13)

Many now feel they are being pulled into the future. We have moved from a changeless past into a relentlessly changing future. This has now caused us to take a more sombre view of the future. The unbridled optimism of the 1950s is gone. We now see a different world. We see unrest in Central Africa and former Yugoslavia, the rise of skinheads in Germany, domestic terrorism, and the breakdown of the central cities. Heilbroner states: 'each of these events, in itself, would have been traumatic, taken together they have hypnotized and horrified the public imagination' (Heilbroner 1995, 70). In the short span of forty years, as we moved from Yesterday to Today, our collective confidence in the future has been shaken. Our confidence and therefore the way we act and perceive our economic future. The expectations formed Today are substantially different from Yesterday. These expectations must be reflected in our models of decision making. Any economic model using Yesterday's assumptions will fail to predict Today's behaviour. Neoclassical theory uses those assumptions. It is no surprise then that Heilbroner makes this very point in 'The Clouded Crystal Ball'. He did not use the terminology of his later work but the thought is identical.

TOMORROW

If the models of Yesterday did not predict Today, then how should we construct a model to envision Tomorrow? Any prediction is a logical extension of trends in the endemic dynamics of the system. What is the endemic dynamic of capitalism? Accumulation. So, if accumulation of capital is what drives the system, we should look at possible restrictions to this process and consequences resulting from this process. We should also examine any perceived changes in the division of power or the market institution. In other words, we must look at the stability in the *nature* and *logic* of the system. Any useful model of our economic future must employ a systemic approach. It must include sociopolitical as well as economic variables. Does Heilbroner's model meet this criteria? Yes. Therefore is his model useful for forecasting our future? Probably. I say probably because if we employ his model of capitalism we implicitly assume the future is a future of capitalism. Using Heilbroner's model would be of little use if socialism were to become the dominant order.

If Heilbroner uses his model to forecast the future, we must assume he believes it is a future of capitalism. While this is true, he thinks it will be a system with a variety of capitalisms. He explains:

> It is likely that capitalism will be the principal form of socioeconomic organization during the twenty-first century, at least for the advanced nations, because no blueprint exists for a viable successor. The attributes of various national capitalisms may differ considerably, one from the other – let us not forget that a capitalist structure has underpinned a gamut of societies from social-democratic Sweden to early fascist Germany and Italy.   (Heilbroner 1995, 100)

The system may have differences but they all will contain the three defining characteristics discussed above (Chapter 5): the division of power, markets and the drive to accumulate.

If we apply the method I mentioned above, what possible problems does Heilbroner see resulting from the accumulation of capital. The first question is can the system continue to accumulate? Can the drive to accumulate sustain the system for ever? The answer is no. He writes:

> Its internal dynamics are too powerful to permit us to imagine the system cruising into the future like a great unsinkable ship. The very essence of a capitalist order is change – technological change, social

and political change, and economic change, as a glance backward in any capitalist nation will make unmistakably evident.

(Heilbroner 1995, 100–1)

This is not a contradiction of his first prediction. He clearly thinks the twenty-first century will see capitalism dominate. However, as we go further into the future the endemic properties of the system will cause it to fail. However, he makes no predictions of when this will occur. It is impossible to tell because capitalism is a system in constant change. Further, it has the ability to self-generate this change.

Capitalism's survival instant is very well developed. Just as it appears to grind to a halt, capitalism experiences 'transformational growth'.[2] This transformational growth is generated from the system's own incentives. New products are introduced which completely transform the way the system interacts. Examples of these would include the introduction of the railroad and the automobile. The key to understanding transformational growth is to appreciate just how large an economic frontier the process opens up. Take the automobile as an example. Not only was a new market opened but it completely changed the existing economic landscape; it changed the distribution method of nearly every other good. Road construction allowed for the creation of suburbs. Hotels, motels and diners sprang up along the newly created roads. Old structures were converted to produce the automobile. It allowed people to live further from their work. In short, transformational growth dispenses what capitalism desperately needs, something to exploit.

A second feature of capitalism's survival response resides in the bifurcation of power. Remember this is a symbiotic relationship. The public realm supports the private by supplying the required infrastructure or producing goods which are necessary but not profitable. It can also refresh markets with policy. Any effort to keep markets 'competitive' adds life to the system. By breaking private monopoly power, public action consistently breaks loose old capital and provides new opportunity. Perhaps the most significant way the public realm may support the private in the future is through closer cooperations such as the European Airbus. The public realm can provide the research and start-up capital when it cannot be generated privately. By providing labour training or systems development, the public realm can manipulate any cost-benefit analysis. The public realm is not bounded by markets or 'business' conditions. It can apply its force to any economic problems. This is a very stabilizing force on the system as a whole. It provides a very large safety net for the entire social order.

Just looking at two of capitalism's many survival mechanisms, it appears that the system can overcome nearly any obstacle. This is not always the case. The true enemies of capitalism are disruptions of the status quo that require responses far outside the anticipated reaction. Heilbroner has discussed many potential problems for capitalism over his career. For our purpose we need only look at a few. I think a representative sample would include: structural unemployment,[3] the system's ability to consistently generate hope, and political adaption to the increasingly global marketplace.

Structural unemployment may be the most serious problem facing the future of the capitalist system. The very nature of transformational growth and new production technologies can remove people from the process. As old industries are displaced by new and capital displaces labour, people are left without the necessary skills to remain employed. Innovation is typically labour-saving. ATM machines replace tellers, computer-driven programs replace telephone operators, middle management is removed when offices become electronic. In a system which relies on the consumption purchases of its labour units the process is devastating. Not only does it cause a decrease in aggregate demand but it also contributes to social unrest. Chronic unemployment causes people to lose faith in the system.

This loss of faith is closely tied to the system's ability to generate hope. Capitalism's expansive nature relies on the participant's belief in a 'profitable' future. To complete the circuit of M–C–M' capital must continually be offered to the system with the belief that profit is generally forthcoming. If this belief is not provided, capitalists stop risking capital and the system comes to a stop. Heilbroner's former Harvard professor, Joseph Schumpeter, (Schumpeter 1942, Chapter 11) traced this scenario. He showed how entrepreneurs would eventually stop venturing capital when the return was gradually reduced. This strikes at the very heart of capitalist accumulation. If structural unemployment or the consistent twenty-year decline in real wages starting in the late 1970s causes an unwillingness to form new capital, then capitalism is in a real crisis.

The last of our enemies of capitalism, political response to global changes in the marketplace, clearly shows how complex the system is becoming. If the political realm is to solve economic problems the polity must have sufficient means. This is not always the case. Heilbroner writes:

> Capitalism is not an easy system to steer under the best of condi-
> tions, and today's unsettling technological trends, increasing eco-

nomic intertwinement and lack of international consensus on economic policy are certainly not the best of conditions.

(Heilbroner 1995, 108)

Any inability of the public realm to help support the system removes a very critical stabilizer. Capital is now footloose around the globe and the national variants of capitalism now compete in daily business. If global capitalism is unable to erect any institutional base which can coordinate the system, the system is in real jeopardy of falling victim to its own internal drives.

The same restraints and supports which underpin national capitalism must also undergird global capitalism. The power of the individual nation-states is consistently eroded as capital moves around the globe. For example, any national policy directed at structural unemployment must be in concert with other capitalist nations around the world. If such a policy made domestic production more expensive, capital would quickly shift to a lower-cost nation. Therefore, it is imperative that the global institutions be developed. This, however, is not an easy prospect. Individual nations are unlikely to willingly submit to mutual restraints. Any internationally coordinated efforts would probably arise only after severe crisis.

Any of these three problems is capable of causing capitalism severe problems. In concert they may be devastating. Therefore, it is useful to complete our method of looking to the future by including three global concerns or parameters. Heilbroner offers this list as a prerequisite for mankind's survival. If capitalism is to survive, it can do so only after careful consideration of the repercussions of violating any of these three larger criteria.

The first is indisputable: 'humankind must achieve a secure terrestrial base for life' (Heilbroner 1995, 116). It can no longer destroy the natural resources it needs to sustain life. The fertility of the air soil must be protected from pollutants. The world will eventually run out of less-developed nations in which we currently dump its waste.

The second criterion addresses the peaceful social environment capitalism needs to function. Civilization must 'find ways to preserve the human community as a whole against its warlike proclivities' (Heilbroner 1995, 117). Civilized society requires order and a structure to work properly.

The last criterion is more elusive. 'The Distant Future must be a time in which the respect for "human nature" is given the cultural and educational centrality it demands' (Heilbroner 1995, 118). If we are to build a more humane civilization in the Distant Future, the inhabitants of that civilization must be informed enough to make reasonable choices. If much behaviour is unconscious human nature, then those motives must be clearly labelled and well understood.

Heilbroner offers these global concerns help in any projection of 'Tomorrow'. It is indicative of his method that he first sketches the boundaries of a future social order. He writes:

> Our purpose is to project a conception of a shape of future things that lies much farther ahead – a distant goal toward which humanity can travel only by long, slow, often errant marches, and whose particulars cannot in any way constitute more than a shimmer of light on the horizon, a half-imagined map of what might some day be our Land of Canaan. As such, its proposals are no more than the first tentative sketch of a social order whose lineament will be a very long time in the making. (Heilbroner 1995, 118–19)

Heilbroner never predicts future specifics. In fact, he does not use the word predict. He generally favours 'future visions' or 'tendencies'. This is not a simple disclaimer. His method of viewing the future is the same as his techniques of viewing the past. It captures the slow unfolding of the system's dynamics. Therefore, any future 'prediction' is an extension of the historical character of capitalism.

It is critical to emphasize that capitalism slowly evolved into its present character. Therefore, any future changes to the capitalist order will likely evolve slowly as well. This is not to say that some external event such as a global war or ecological catastrophe could not change the future quickly and radically. What is important is the response to such an event. Capitalism could be replaced quickly if the reaction takes the place of a long-term government control or military organization. If the drive for accumulation is replaced with a more immediate survival instinct, the careful counterbalances of the capitalist order could quickly collapse. This is the reason for Heilbroner's global criteria. He adds the necessary conditions for possibly avoiding these external threats and then projects the future inertia of capitalism. The cultural and institutional underpinnings of the system itself project the responses to external stimuli and the past contains examples of these responses. Heilbroner warns that not learning history's lessons can result in a very painful mistake (Heilbroner 1993a, Chapter 7).

7 A Final Appraisal

The time has come to review the main points of Heilbroner's economic method. Let me begin with an innocent question. Is Heilbroner an economist? If we define an economist as one who practices the science of 'economics' the answer is no. He certainly does not employ the standard methods of the modern science of economics. We have previously seen that Heilbroner openly questions the relevance of this approach. In fact he has gone as far as saying economic science can actually veil any true understanding of the problems. The typical methods employed by the profession direct our attention to the symptoms of the economic problem and not the cause. Surface price fluctuations are an epiphenomenon; the real problems lie below the surface. The real problems reside deep within the *nature* and *logic* of the capitalist system. However, while Heilbroner is not an economist who is cut from the same cloth as modern reductionist theorists, he is an *economist* in that he is a practitioner of 'political economy'.

This chapter opens with a comparison of Heilbroner's work to traditional schools of thought. Specifically, it points out the affinity between his work and the Old Institutionalist School (OIE). It highlights the similarities in approach and scope with the work of men like Veblen and Ayres. It examines the temporal properties of institution formation highlighted by Ayres and Veblen. It then traces these through the work of Heilbroner. We find that Heilbroner's work meets all the criteria of the OIE. The chapter closes with a brief review of those who have had the most influence on Heilbroner's work. In particular, we return to the long relationship between Heilbroner and Adolph Lowe.

HEILBRONER AS INSTITUTIONALIST

One of the difficulties in fully appreciating Heilbroner's work is his lack of association with any formal school of thought. His work shares common elements with many but he never makes any personal association. The best way to begin is to specify his general approach to the study of the economy. We will open with his views of the capitalist order and his definition of economics.

Seeing capitalism as a regime is essential to understanding Heil-broner's economics. Once capitalism is seen as a social formation with a distinct history and sense of purpose, we begin to understand the fundamentals of material provisioning. Viewing capitalism simply as a market system or business society we automatically limit ourselves to seeing only part of the process. It is the inclusion of the social and political dimension that truly defines Heilbroner's economic vision. When he states that economics must be approached as 'a form of systematized power and of the socialized beliefs by which that power is depicted as a natural and necessary form of social life' (Heilbroner 1992a, 247), he is clearly referring to the institutional substructure which undergirds capitalism.

The endemic institutional focus in Heilbroner's work makes it tempting to label him an institutionalist. If we use the criteria set by Walton H. Hamilton in 1919 (Hamilton 1919), it is clear that Heilbroner's work is certainly institutionalist in nature. Hamilton defines the scope of institutional economics as the explanation of economic order in the face of a variety of economic phenomena (Hamilton 1919, 311). He lays down five criteria which define institu-tionalist thought.

The first criterion is that *economic theory should unify the science*. In other words, theory should have a holistic approach. It must allow a more comprehensive understanding of the economic process. Hamil-ton warns against subdividing economics into small subfields. He believes this practice limits the understanding of the economic process. Economics cannot be useful in this format. Hamilton writes:

> As a result economics today tends to break up into a large number of overlapping but unrelated inquiries and to lose the unity which in times past has been its source of strength.   (Hamilton 1919, 312)

Heilbroner would certainly agree with this statement. His worldly philosophers' scenarios are a comprehensive model of the economic process and his 'veil' is the description of this fragmented focus of modern economists.

Hamilton's second criterion is that *economic theory should be relev-ant to the modern problem of control*. Control is defined as the sense of providing motion to the economic process. Economic investigation must therefore focus on the systemic inertia and cultural constraints that control and shape provisioning. This is found throughout Heil-broner's work as well as Adolph Lowe's. In Heilbroner and Lowe, behavioural, motivational and order patterns abound; they are the fundamental dynamics of the system.

The third criterion is *The proper subject-matter of economic theory is institutions*. This, of course, is fundamental to Heilbroner's work. His definition of economics details that capitalism is built on a core of internalized institutions and core values. It is the interactions within this core of institutions which shape and control the economic process. This is the background for Heilbroner's sociopolitical investigations.

The final two criteria, *economic theory is concerned with matters of process* and *economics must be based on an acceptable theory of human behaviour*, significantly define Heilbroner as an institutionalist. It is obvious that his work is deeply concerned with process and human behaviour. In fact, Heilbroner's economics *is* the study of the process of human provisioning through history. It rests on the process of accumulation and the behavioural properties of depth psychology.

Can we define Heilbroner as an institutionalist given these five criteria? The answer must be yes. His work clearly conforms to all five of Hamilton's criteria and it embodies the holistic orientation of original institutionalist (OIE) thought. His methods also fit with more contemporary institutionalists. His definition of economics as the study of power allocation aligns him with the work of J. K. Galbraith. Further, his holistic methodology also links Heilbroner with contemporary institutionalists. We will examine each in turn.

Power and the process of integrating the power beliefs into the prevailing culture is beyond what most (excluding institutionalists) would consider to be 'economics'. Like Heilbroner, Galbraith incorporates power into his economic model. He similarly believes that economics must confront the drive for power and understand why people want it (Galbraith 1967, xiv). It is, however, just as important to understand why individuals willingly acquiesce to market forces as it is to describe those market forces. The 'market' is nothing but a collection of socially internalized beliefs about the proper methods of exchange. Heilbroner approaches market economics with the same *élan* as Marx did the commodity. If Marx described the commodity as a 'social hieroglyphic' which is an invisible container of social relationships, then Heilbroner encapsulates all socioeconomic relations under his definition of 'capitalist economics'. I use the term *capitalist* economics to emphasize the fact that Heilbroner does not believe social formations prior to capitalism is the proper study of economics. He is quick to say that all societies had their economic activities, but they were never sufficiently distinct from other social functions for economics to be of much use. Therefore, economics can only be the study of capitalism.

As we have seen, this approach dissents from that employed by most traditional economists. At the heart of this dissent is the fundamental methodology Heilbroner employs. Heilbroner does not use a 'positivist' approach in his inquiry. Rather, he works with what is best described as a *hermeneutic* methodology. Where the traditional positivist methodology emphasizes the detailing of *observed* behaviour, hermeneutics emphasizes the understanding of *all* behaviour. Observed behaviour is the result of ingrained behavioural tendencies, therefore, if we identify these tendencies, we are already privy to the resulting behaviours. In economic systems where the reporting of economic events is always delayed, this is a critical difference. This could be very beneficial in forecasting future economic conditions. If economic policy making has been described as driving a car using only the rear view mirror, then this endemic forward-looking technique is useful.

This forward-looking benefit is somewhat of a moot point in Heilbroner's projections. Without question, the delay of a quarter or two is harmful in forecasting economic conditions. However, when Heilbroner's taxonomy describes the Distant Past as encompassing 150 000 years, a quarter or two delay does not appear particularly malicious. In fact, Keynes's famous phrase may have to be amended to: 'In the *short* run we are all dead!'

VEBLEN AND AYRES

Heilbroner may limit himself by not emphasizing a closer identification with the institutionalist school. The institutionalists were clearly working in his chosen areas well before he wrote *The Worldly Philosophers*. Of particular importance is the institutionalist's relationship between time and the formation of institutions. C. E. Ayres and Thorstein Veblen wrote at considerable length on this topic. Like Heilbroner, Ayres and Veblen viewed the economic process within historical time. They both emphasized the temporal element in the formation of institutions. As Heilbroner writes of the future tendencies of the capitalist order, he is mirroring Veblen–Ayres past-binding and forward-looking institutions (Ayres 1944 [1962]). As the capitalist process unfolds, the past-binding (ceremonial) institutions create a drag on the system. It creates a drag but also a continuity, in accepted ways of acting. Heilbroner's 'Tradition' economies exhibit this type of structure. The

forward-looking (instrumental)[1] institutions such as developed technological structures help propel the system into the future. It is the
combination or tension between these which helps hold the capitalist
structure together. The ceremonial aspects provide established ways of
doing things in the face of changes caused by the instrumental elements.

Heilbroner is clearly operating within the tradition of the institutionalist school. However, he tends to cite and side with those who are
from his past or have some association with the New School. This, I
am sure, is more a matter of convenience and loyalty than any predetermined bias.

In all Heilbroner's work it is easy to see the influence of his mentors.
The list is pretty impressive. It includes the immediate names of: Alvin
Hansen, Joseph Schumpeter, Adolph Lowe, Paul Sweezy. Further, as a
historian of economic thought, he was significantly influenced by his
'Worldly Philosophers': Adam Smith, Karl Marx, David Ricardo,
Thomas Malthus, Alfred Marshall and Thorstein Veblen. This list
must be the preeminent who's who in political economy. I would
doubt that many would quibble with the pedigree of those on the list.
The important thing to notice here is the general untouchable nature of
those on the list. Modern economists may disagree with the various
theories presented, but few attack the scholarship.

The early association of Heilbroner with his 'Worldly Philosophers'
is one secret to Heilbroner's success. All of his views, right or wrong,
carry the collective weight of Smith, Marx, Ricardo, Malthus, Keynes
and Veblen. Being the creator of *The Worldly Philosophers* is a very
valuable self-generated gift. Perhaps more than the acclaim of their
work, Heilbroner has benefited from their broad range of visions. The
scenarios they constructed are of the same scope as his capitalist realm.
The work of Smith and Marx is highly sociopolitical in nature like
Heilbroner's.

AGAIN, ADOLPH LOWE

In this concluding section, we must re-emphasize the enormous influence of Adolph Lowe. Although the development of their work did not
parallel each other, much of Lowe's thought is so deeply ingrained in
Heilbroner's that it is sometimes difficult to distinguish between the
two. Trace any theme in Heilbroner's economics and you will find
something of Lowe. If we were to detail a few of Lowe's contributions,

I believe we would have to start with his 1935 book *Economics and Sociology: A Plea For Co-operation in the Social Sciences*. Heilbroner's holistic approach to the study of capitalism is a mirror of Lowe. In 1935 Lowe wrote: 'The whole idea of an autonomous economic science can only arise, if there are "economic" elements in human behavior which are not necessarily "social"' (Lowe 1935, 41–2). Thus, the sterile abstractions of neoclassical theory may be of little use if social aspects influenced economic behaviour. This is his plea for the cooperation of economics and sociology. Lowe, like Heilbroner, believed there was a distinct sociopolitical nature to economics and the simple Robinson Crusoe abstractions of the neoclassicals may not capture it. He believed 'every real economic action is always part of man's social activity, and that Robinson Crusoe though logically conceivable is historically unreal... any economic system is embedded in a society' (Lowe 1935, 46). Karl Polanyi would popularize the 'embedded economy' some years later in *The Great Transformation*.

Another significant influence on Heilbroner is Lowe's idea of economic order. The reliance of macroeconomic order on micro-unit's behavioural patterns can be seen throughout Heilbroner's work. It provides the foundation of Heilbroner's questioning of the future of worldly philosophy. It also runs throughout all of Heilbroner's scenarios for the future. If economic society is beginning to drift toward disorder like Lowe suggests, then any economic predictions have no valid grounding. Heilbroner incorporates Lowe's instrumental method into his visions of the future by suggesting the explicit role of government in the economy.

Heilbroner has always been an advocate of government and private interactions. He even speaks of a 'Slightly Imaginary Sweden' as a hypothetical goal. It provides an example of a socio-democratic capitalism that easily blends public and private enterprises. It is an attempt to couple the forward motion of capitalist economy with a more human-centred life. He believes the successful capitalisms of the future will be of this pattern.

The last significant influence of Lowe I wish to mention, is the parallel between his formation of 'macro-goals' and Heilbroner's method of 'future related understanding'. Both Heilbroner and Lowe form their future scenarios from a very sociopolitical orientation. This stems from their belief that modern capitalism is becoming more political and less autonomous. Heilbroner's idea of the worldly philosophy failing because of the inclusion of more political direction, directly leads to Lowe's instrumental method of achieving, macro-goals. Lowe writes:

> Though I leave no doubt that the instrumental method is applicable to the elaboration of the means suitable to the attainment of *any* macro-goal, be it the size distribution and composition of aggregate output, the level of resource utilization, the rate of growth, or the order of distribution, I have confined the practical test cases to two: full utilization of resources, and balanced growth. But my choice was ultimately determined by political considerations. There are the only macro-goals which, I believe, are fully compatible with the institutional environment of mature capitalism.   (Lowe 1969, 35)

The formation of usable macro-goals relies on the proper understanding of the current system. This is the foundation of Heilbroner's method of future related understanding. If we understand the future tendencies inherent in the system we can then formulate proper and achievable macro-goals. The continuing encroachment of the public realm can only be tempered by defining a proper role for government. If it is to stay involved, it must be enlarged from the traditional role of mediator. The public and private realms must increase their overt cooperation. The covert separation of power and symbiotic relationship between public and private has, by definition, made the two partners in the capitalist system. The truly successful capitalisms will be the ones which exploit this relationship and not try to hide it.

To conclude, let me return to my question: Is Heilbroner an economist? We know that his is far from a traditional modern economics. The mathematical and statistical shades of modern theory are simply not part of Heilbroner's work. We have seen that much of Heilbroner's work could easily be classified as Institutionalist. Is this the best classification? Probably not. Heilbroner's work shares common elements with many schools of thought. At various times he writes like a Keynesian, Marxist, Institutionalist, post-Keynesian and neo-Marxist. I do not believe this to be a contradiction. I believe his inclusion of many school's elements make his writings accessible to such a wide audience inside, as well as outside, the economics profession.

Heilbroner's most significant contribution to the discipline of 'economics' is likely his work in the history of economic thought. *The Worldly Philosophers* is regarded as the standard text for the introduction to history of thought. He is recognized as an eminent scholar of

Smith and Schumpeter. He has written extensively on the evolution of the methodology of economic analysis and public debt.

However, it is perhaps his contributions outside academia that are his most significant. His books have demystified economics for a generation of readers. His prose is elegant and easily understood. He brings an economic perspective to social inquiry that is all too often absent. Today's economic writers often forget that the reader does not often possess formal training. Heilbroner's work strikes to the heart of economic problems with little or no jargon and his socio-political focus helps shed light on the true socio-economic problems.

In summary, the depth and breadth of his work is unmatched by any contemporary economist. His contributions lie within the science of economics, and perhaps more importantly, in the related fields of sociology and economic history. He has made economics a less mysterious subject to educated laymen. His considerable understanding of the capitalist economy allows him to take a very wide view of the economic problem. Whether he admits it or not, he is a modern-day Worldly Philosopher.

Notes

2 THE MAN AND HIS VISION

1. *Current Biography*, 1975, p. 188.
2. Heilbroner has used this term in a number of places. The best explanations of its meaning would be included in interviews in *Business Week* (September 30, 1972) and *Psychology Today* (February 1975).
3. Paul Sweezy was Heilbroner's 'section man' in his sophomore year. Sweezy would become one of America's leading Marxist economists. Heilbroner says that Sweezy interested him 'enormously in the social overtones of economics' (Van Dyne 1978, 4).
4. After the death of his wife Bea in 1982, Lowe soon returned to the northern city of Wolfenbüttel to live near his daughter.
5. See the preface of the 1986 edition of *The Worldly Philosophers* for the complete story.
6. See Sidney Hook's review in *Commentary*.
7. It can be argued that books he wrote in the 1970s addressed questions of a Marxist style. Most were inquires on the economic and social order, or looked at the consequences of a social order.
8. See Chapter 3 for a more comprehensive treatment of Heilbroner's hermeneutic approach to economics.

3 LIMITATIONS OF TRADITIONAL ECONOMICS

1. See Robbins 1949, Chapter 1.
2. This essay originally appeared in The *New York Review of Books* (December 5, 1968) and later, in a slightly different form, in *Between Capitalism and Socialism* (1970) under the title 'Marxism and the Economic Establishment'.
3. The role of expectations is only a small part of Lowe's model.
4. See the opening pages of *Behind The Veil of Economics: Essays in the Worldly Philosophy*.
5. Mumpsimus is a term employed by Joan Robinson which means 'persistence in a belief one knows to be mistaken'. Heilbroner is convinced she unearthed this in an English crossword (Heilbroner 1973, 136).

4 THE METHODOLOGY OF WORDLY PHILOSOPHY

1. I am using 'ism' to refer to the taxonomic label associated with the doctrine of a given social order.
2. See Keynes's 'The Council of Four,' Paris, 1919, in *Essays in Biography*.

3. There are several heterodox schools who are currently using methods which would be completely compatible with the worldly philosophy approach. Institutionalists, post-Keynesians and neo-Marxists would fall into this category.
4. Leonardo believed that 'the mirror is our master'. He believed mirrors should be used to achieve an expanded visual fidelity in painting.
5. This is not to imply that Heilbroner writes in the methodological individualist tradition. To be sure he does not. He is, however, sensitive to the fundamentals of human behaviour when formulating his analysis.
6. This is again the influence of Heilbroner's mentor Adolph Lowe.
7. Affect is a rather ambiguous term which is universally accepted as referring to the psychological capacity for identification, trust, sympathy and love. Heilbroner expands this definition in the first chapter of *Behind the Veil*.
8. Human element, sociopolitical element and economic element.

5 THE STRUCTURE OF CAPITALISM

1. See Lester Thurow's 1996 book *The Future of Capitalism: How Today's Economic Forces Shape Tomorrow's World*. New York: Morrow.
2. See Joseph Schumpeter, *Theory of Economic Development*.
3. This implicitly excludes worker cooperatives and similar worker-owned businesses.
4. Macro-order as demonstrated by Adolph Lowe in *On Economic Knowledge*.
5. It is more likely that the success of books like *The Future as History* and *Human Prospect* has given Heilbroner a reputation of social guru.
6. See Chapter 2.

6 A VIEW TO THE FUTURE

1. It is no coincidence that 1974 also marked the publication of his *An Inquiry Into the Human Prospect*.
2. Heilbroner discusses transformational technologies but not transformational growth. For a more detailed description of transformational growth see the work of Edward J. Nell. I have listed several of the seminal works in the bibliography.
3. This is only one aspect of the much larger issue of income distribution.

7 A FINAL APPRAISAL

1. This is not 'instrumental' in the Lowe context. This instrumental refers to the tradition established by Dewey.

The Economic Writings of Robert Heilbroner

BOOKS

1953. *The Worldly Philosophers: The Lives, Times and Ideas of the Great Economic Thinkers*, 6th edn. New York: Touchstone.

1956. *The Quest for Wealth*. New York: Simon & Schuster.

1959. *The Future as History: The Historic Currents of Our Time and the Direction in Which They are Taking America*. New York: Harper & Row. Rpt Harper Torchbooks, 1967.

1962. *The Making of Economic Society*. Englewood Cliffs, NJ: Prentice-Hall.

1963. *The World of Economics*. American Library Association (pamphlet).

1963. *The Great Ascent: The Struggle for Economic Development in Our Time*. New York: Harper & Row.

1963. *A Primer on Government Spending*. New York: Random House.

1965. *The Limits of American Capitalism*. New York: W. W. Norton.

1965. *Understanding Macroeconomics*. Englewood Cliffs, NJ: Prentice Hall.

1966. *Automation in the Perspective of Long-Term Technological Change*. US Department of Labor, (pamphlet).

1968. *Understanding Microeconomics*. Englewood Cliffs, NJ: Prentice-Hall.

1968. *The Economic Problem*. Englewood Cliffs, NJ: Prentice-Hall.

1969. *Economic Means and Social Ends*. Englewood Cliffs, NJ: Prentice-Hall (ed.).

1970. *Between Capitalism and Socialism: Essays in Political Economics*. New York: Vintage.

1971. *Economic Relevance: A Second Look*. Pacific Palisades, California: Goodyear.

1972. *In the Name of Profit*. New York: Doubleday.

1974. *An Inquiry into the Human Prospect*. New York: W. W. Norton.

1975. *Corporate Social Policy: Selections from Business and Society Review*. Reading Massachusetts: Addison-Wesley.

1976. *Business Civilization in Decline*. New York: W. W. Norton.

1976. *The Economic Transformation of America*. New York: Harcourt Brace Jovanovich.

1978. *Beyond Boom and Crash*. New York: W. W. Norton.

1980. *Marxism: For and Against*. New York: W. W. Norton.

1981. *Five Economic Challenges*. Englewood Cliffs, NJ: Prentice-Hall.

1982. *Economics Explained*. New York: Touchstone (with Lester Thurow).

1985.   *The Act of Work*. Library of Congress, Washington.
1985.   *The Nature and Logic of Capitalism*. New York: W. W. Norton.
1986.   *The Essential Adam Smith*. New York: W. W. Norton.
1988.   *Behind the Veil of Economics*. New York: W. W. Norton.
1989.   *The Debt and Deficit: False Alarms, Real Possibilities*. New York: W. W. Norton.
1993.   *21st Century Capitalism*. New York: W. W. Norton.
1995.   *Visions of the Future: The Distant Past, Yesterday, Today, Tomorrow*. New York: Oxford University Press.
1996.   *The Crisis of Vision in Modern Economic Thought*. Cambridge: Cambridge University Press.
1996.   *Teachings From The Worldly Philosophy*. New York: W. W. Norton.

CHAPTERS IN BOOKS

1953.   'The American Poor', *Man and Modern Society*, K. De Schweinetz and K. W. Thompson (eds), New York: Holt.
1957.   'Communicating Economic Research: As a Writer Sees It', *Report on the Conference on Communicating Economic Research*. Hanover, New Hampshire: Amos Tuck School.
1962.   'The Impact of Technology: The Historic Debate', *Automation and Technological Change*. (American Assembly), Englewood Cliffs, NJ: Prentice-Hall.
1964.   'The View from the Top: Reflections on a Changing Business Ideology', *The Business Establishment*, E. Cheit (ed.), New York: Wiley.
1966.   'Which Goals for the Future?', *Manpower Policies for Youth*, National Committee on Employment of Youth, E. Cohen and L. Kapp (eds), New York: Columbia University Press.
1968.   'Counter-revolutionary America', *A Dissenter's Guide to Foreign Policy*, Irving Howe (ed.), New York: Praeger.
1968.   'The Eye of the Needle', *Moral Man and Economic Enterprise*, Evanston, Illinois: Northwestern University Press.
1971.   'On the Limited Relevance of Economics', *Capitalism Today*, Daniel Bell and Irving Kristol (eds), New York: Basic Books.
1971.   'The Roots of Neglect in the United States', *Is Law Dead?*, E. V. Rostow (ed.), New York: Simon & Schuster.
1972.   'Do Machines Make History', *Technology and Culture*, M. Kranzberg and W. H. Davenport (eds), New York: Schocken Books. Reprinted in *Technological Determinism Revisited*.
1974.   'Adam Smith', *Encyclopedia Britannica*.
1975.   'The Paradox of Progress: Decline and Decay in the Wealth of Nations', *Essays on Adam Smith*, A. S. Skinner and T. Wilson (eds), New York: Oxford.
1981.   'Was Schumpeter Right?', *Schumpeter's Vision*, A. Heertje (ed.), New York: Praeger.

1982.   'What is Socialism', *Beyond the Welfare State*, Irving Howe (ed.), New York: Schocken Books.

1983.   'John D. Rockefeller', *Historical Viewpoints*, John Garraty (ed.), New York: Harper & Row.

1984.   'Capitalism as Gestalt: A Contrast of Visions', *Free Market Conservatism*, Edward Nell (ed.), London: George Allen & Unwin.

1984.   'The Nature and Logic of Capitalism According to Adam Smith', *Beschäftigung, Verteilung und Konjunktur*, Festschrift für Adolph Lowe, Bremen: Universität Bremen.

1986.   'Economics and Political Economy: Marx, Keynes and Schumpeter', *Marx, Schumpeter and Keynes: A Centenary Celebration of dissent*, Suzanne Helburn and David Bramhall (eds), Armonk, NY: M. E. Sharpe.

1986.   'Realities and Appearances in Capitalism', *Corporations and the Common Good*, Robert B. Dickie and Leroy S. Rouner (eds), Notre Dame, Ind.: University of Notre Dame Press.

1988.   'Wealth', *The New Palgrave*, John Eatwell, Murray Milgate and Peter Newman (eds), New York and London: Macmillan.

1988.   'Capitalism', *The New Palgrave*, John Eatwell, Murray Milgate and Peter Newman (eds), New York and London: Macmillan.

1988.   'Rhetoric and Ideology', *The Consequences of Economic Rhetoric*, A. Klamer, D. McCloskey and R. Solow (eds), New York: Cambridge University Press.

1990.   'Economics as Ideology', *Economics as Discourse*, Warren Samuels (ed.), Boston: Kluwer.

1990.   'The Future of Capitalism', *Sea-Changes: American Foreign Policy in a World Transformed*, Nicolas X. Rizopoulos (ed.), New York: Council on Foreign Relations Press.

1991.   'Economic Systems', *Encyclopedia Britannica*.

1993.   'Socialism', *The Fortune Encyclopedia of Economics*, in David Henderson (ed.), New York: Warner Books.

Forth.   'Technological Determinism Revisited', in Merrit Roe Smith (ed.), MIT Press, forthcoming.

Forth.   'The Economic View of Progress', in *The Idea of Progress Revisited*, Leo Marx and Bruce Mazlish (eds) forthcoming.

ARTICLES

1942.   'Saving and Investment: Dynamic Aspects', *American Economic Review*. December 1942.

1950.   'The American Poor', *Harper's Magazine*. June 1950, pp. 27–33.

1952.   'Labour Unrest in the British Nationalized Sector', *Social Research*. March 1952.

1960.   'Epitaph for the Steel Master', *American Heritage*. August 1960.

1962.   'The Revolution of Economic Development', *American Scholar*. Autumn.

1963.   'Transcendental Capitalism', *The New York Review of Books*. Vol. I, No. 2, 1963.

1963.   'Innocence Abroad.' *Commentary*. February 1963.

1964.   'The Share-the-Tax Plan', *The New York Times Sunday Magazine*. December 27, 1964.

1966.   'A Marxist America', *The New York Review of Books*. May 26, 1966.

1966.   'Is Economic Theory Possible?', *Social Research*. Summer 1966.

1967.   'Capitalism Without Tears', *The New York Review of Books*. June 29, 1967.

1968.   'Who's Running This Show?', *The New York Review of Books*. January 4, 1968.

1968.   'Rhetoric and Reality in the Struggle Between Business and the State', *Social Research*. Autumn 1968.

1968.   'Making a Rational Foreign Policy Now', *Harper's Magazine*. September 1968.

1968.   'Futurology', *The New York Review of Books*. September 26, 1968.

1968.   'Putting Marx to Work', *The New York Review of Books*. December 5, 1968.

1969.   'Marxism: For and Against', *The New York Review of Books*. June 5, 1969.

1969.   'Reflections on the Future of Socialism', *Commentary*. November 1969.

1970.   'On the Limits of Economic Prediction', *Diogenes*. April 1970.

1970.   'Ecological Armageddon', *The New York Review of Books*. April 23, 1970.

1970.   'On the Limited Relevance of Economics', *Public Interest*. Fall 1970.

1970.   'On the Possibility of a Political Economics', *Journal of Economic Issues*. December 1970.

1971.   'The Multinational Corporation and the Nation State', *The New York Review of Books*. February 11, 1971.

1972.   'A Radical View of Socialism', *Social Research*. Spring 1972.

1972.   'Ecological "Balance" and the "Stationary" State' (with Jack Allentuck), *Land Economics*. August 1972.

1972.   'Growth and Survival', *Foreign Affairs*. October 1972.

1973.   'The Paradox of Progress: Decline and Decay in the Wealth of Nations', *Journal of the History of Ideas*. April 1973.

1973.   'Economic Problems of a Post-Industrial Society', *Dissent*. Spring 1973.

1973.   'Economics as a "Value Free" Science', *Social Research*. Spring 1973.

1974.   'The Clouded Crystal Ball', *American Economic Review*. May 1974.

1975.   'Marxism, Psychoanalysis and the Problem of a Unified Theory of Behavior', *Social Research*. Autumn 1975.

1976.   'What is the Human Prospect', *The New York Review of Books*. January 24, 1976.

1976.   'Homage to Adam Smith', *Challenge*. March–April 1976.

1976.   'Boom and Crash', *The New Yorker*. August 28, 1976.
1976.   'Middle Class Myths: Middle Class Realities', *Atlantic*. October 1976.
1978.   'Inescapable Marx', *The New York Review of Books*. June 29, 1978.
1979.   'Modern Economics as a Chapter in the History of Economic Thought', *History of Political Economy*. Vol. 11, No. 2, 1979; also included in Mark Blaug (ed.) *The Historiography of Economics*. Aldershot: Edward Elgar, 1991.
1979.   'Inflationary Capitalism', *The New Yorker*. October 8, 1979.
1980.   'The Inflation in Your Future', *The New York Review of Books*. May 1, 1980.
1980.   'Adolph Lowe', *Journal of Economic Issues*. June 1980.
1981.   'The Demand for the Supply Side', *The New York Review of Books*. June 11, 1981.
1982.   'The Socialization of the Individual in Adam Smith', *History of Political Economy*. Vol.50, No. 2, 1982.
1983.   'The Problem of Value in the Constitution of Economic Thought', *Social Research*. Summer 1983.
1983.   'Economic Prospects', *The New Yorker*. August 29, 1983 (first prize, Gerald R. Loeb Awards for Distinguished Financial and Business Journalism).
1984.   'Economics and Political Economy: Marx, Keynes and Schumpeter', *Journal of Economic Issues*. September 1984.
1985.   'The State and Capitalism: How They Interact and Move Apart', *Dissent*. Fall 1985.
1987.   'Fundamental Economic Concepts – Another Perspective', *Journal of Economic Education*. Spring 1987.
1987.   'Perceptions and Misperceptions: How Economists and the Public See Economics – and Each Other', *Journal of Economic and Monetary Affairs*, Middlebury VT., International Institute for Economic Advancement. July 1987.
1987.   'Hard Times', *The New Yorker*. September 14, 1987 (first prize, Gerald R. Loeb Awards).
1988.   'The Coming Meltdown of Traditional Capitalism', *Ethics and International Affairs*. Vol. 2, 1988.
1988.   'Vision and Ideology', *Dissent*. Spring 1988.
1988.   'How I Learned to Love the Deficit' *The New York Times*. September 4, 1988.
1988.   'Is America Falling Behind: An Interview of Paul Kennedy', *American Heritage*. September/October 1988.
1989.   'The Triumph of Capitalism', *The New Yorker*. January 23, 1989.
1989.   'All Rich Nations Need Their Debt', *The Nation*. January 23, 1989.
1989.   'Abolishing the Deficit', *Challenge*, May/June 1989.
1989.   'Examining Stein's Proposals', *Challenge*. July/August 1989.
1989.   'A Tune-Up For the Market', *The New York Times Magazine*. September 24, 1989.
1989.   'The Great Question', *American Heritage*. December, 1989.

1989.	'Rereading the Affluent Society', *Journal of Economic Issues*. June 1989.
1990.	'Seize the Day', *The New York Review of Books*. February 15, 1990.
1990.	'Rethinking the Past, Rehoping the Future', *Social Research*. Fall 1990.
1990.	'After Communism', *The New Yorker*. September 10, 1990.
1990.	'The World After Communism', *Dissent*. Fall 1990.
1990.	'Analysis and Vision in the History of Modern Economic Thought', *Journal of Economic Literature*. September 1990.
1991.	'Was the Right Right All Along', *Harper's Magazine*. January 1991.
1991.	'Economics as Universal Science', *Social Research*. Summer 1991.
1991.	'Economic Predictions', *The New Yorker*. July 8, 1991.
1991.	'Rough Roads to Capitalism', *The New York Times*. September 15, 1991.
1991.	'Thoughts on the Triumph of Capitalism', *The American Prospect*. Fall 1991.
1991.	'Lifting the Silent Depression', *The New York Review of Books*. October 23, 1991.
1991.	'From Sweden to Socialism', *Dissent*. Winter 1991.
1992.	'The Deficit', *Nation*. January 27, 1992.
1992.	'The Myth of a Savings Shortage', *The American Prospect*. Spring 1992.
1992.	'How to Restore U.S. Economic Momentum', *Institutional Investor*. May 1992.
1992.	'The Deficit: A Way Out', *The New York Review of Books*. October 22, 1992.
1992.	'An Economy in Deep Trouble', *Dissent*. Fall 1992.
1992.	'History's Lessons', *Social Research*. Winter 1992.
1992.	'Is a Worldly Philosophy Still Possible? Adolph Lowe as Analyst and Visionary', *Review of Social Economy*. Winter 1992.
1992.	'We Have the Vision to Get U.S. Moving', *Los Angeles Times*. May 15, 1992.
1992.	'Create Two Budgets', *The New York Times*. June 10, 1992.
1993.	'Anti-Depression Economics', *Atlantic Monthly*. April 1993.
1993.	'The Case for Hope: Clinton's 100 Days and Beyond', *The Nation*. May 10, 1993.
1993.	'Was Schumpeter Right After All?', *Journal of Economic Perspectives*. Summer.
1993.	'Does Socialism Have a Future?', *The Nation*. September 27, 1993.
1994.	'Vision in Economic Thought', *Journal of Economic Issues*. June 1994 (receipt of the Veblen–Commons Award)

INTERVIEWS/PROFILES (PARTIAL LISTING)

| 1974. | Hearings before the Subcommittee on the Environment, House of Representatives, June 4, 1974. Serial No. 93–55, pp. 33–51. National Energy Conservation Act of 1974. |

1960. *Saturday Review of Literature*, April 2, 1960.
1960. *American Historical Review*, July 1960.
1962. *New York Herald Tribune Books*, August 19, 1962.
1967. *The New York Times Book Review*, October 28, 1967.
1967. *Contemporary Authors*, rev. edn, vols 1–4 1967.
1972. *New York Post*, February 21, 1972.
1972. *Business Week*, September 30, 1972.
1974. Bill Moyers' Journal, *WNET* interview, April 23, 1974.
1974. *Science*, August 16, 1974.
1974. *Who's Who in America*, 1974–1975.
1974. *New Republic*, March 30, 1974.
1974. *Time*, April 1974.
1975. *Psychology Today*, February 1975.
1976. *Current Biography*, H. H. Wilson Co., June 1976.
1976. *US News and World Report*, March 8, 1976.
1978. *Chronicle of Higher Education*, October 16, 1978.
1980. *Public Opinion*, April/May 1980.
1980. *The New York Times Book Review*, April 13, 1980.
1980. *Commentary*, July 1980.
1981. *Contemporary Authors* New Revision Series, 4, 1981.
1982. *Challenge*, October/November 1982.
1984. Heertje, Arnold. *The U.S.A. in the World Economy*. (San Francisco: Freeman, Cooper & Co., 1984, pp. 58–67.
1987. *Contemporary Authors*. New Revision Series, Volume 21, 1987.
1988. Okroi, Loren J. *Galbraith, Harrington, Heilbroner: Economics and Dissent in an Age of Optimism*. Princeton, NJ: Princeton University Press, 1988.
1988. *Who's Who in America 1988–1989*.
1989. *New Perspectives Quarterly*, 'The Triumph of Capitalism', Fall 1989.
1991. *World Authors*, 1980–1985, H. H. Wilson Co., 1991, pp. 402–5.
1991. *Forbes Magazine*, May 27, 1991.
1992. *A Biographical Dictionary of Dissenting Economists*, eds Phillip Arestis and Malcolm Sawyer. Cheltenham: Edward Elgar, 1992.
1993. *New Perspective Quarterly*, 'The Rest of the World (ROW): Off the Track', Spring 1993.

REVIEWS (PARTIAL LISTING)

1954. 'Review of *History of Economic Analysis*, by Joseph Schumpeter.' *The Nation*, April 17, 1954.
1964. 'Review of *The Politics of Hysteria*, edited by Edmund Stillman and William Pfaff.' *The New York Review of Books*, February 20, 1964.
1965. 'Review of *The Meaning of the 20th Century*, by Kenneth Boulding.' *Book Week*, January 17, 1965.
1970. 'Review of *Pentagon Capitalism*, by Seymour Melman.' *New York Review*, July 23, 1970.

1971.   'Review of *Politics and the Stages of Growth*, by W. W. Rostow.'
          The New York Times Book Review, August 1, 1971.
1972.   'Review of *Alienation: Marx's Conception of Man in Capitalist
          Society* by Bertell Ollman and *Alienation and Economics* by Walter
          Weisskopf.' *The New York Review of Books*, March 9, 1972.
1972.   'Review of "Radical Economics: A Review Essay"'. *American
          Political Science Review*, September 1972.
1972.   'Review of *Reflections in the Causes of Human Misery*, by Barring-
          ton Moore.' *The New York Review of Books*, October 5, 1972.
1973.   'Review of *America and the World Political Economy*, by David P.
          Calleo and Benjamin Rowland.' *The New York Review of Books*,
          November 29, 1973.
1975.   'Review of *Labor and Monopoly Capital*, by Harry Braverman.' *The
          New York Review of Books*, January 23, 1975.
1975.   'Review of "Kenneth Boulding, Collected Papers: A Review Arti-
          cle"' *Journal of Economic Issues*, March 1975.
1978.   'Review of *Politics and Markets*, by Charles E. Lindblom.' *The New
          York Times Book Review*, February 19, 1978.
1980.   'Review of *Free to Choose: A Personal Statement*, by Milton and
          Rose Friedman.' *The New York Review of Books*, April 17, 1980.
1980.   'Review of *A Guide to Post Keynesian Economics*, by Alfred Eich-
          ner.' *The New York Review of Books*, April 17, 1980.
1982.   'Review of *Essays in Trespassing and Shifting Involvements*, by
          Albert Hirschman.' *The New York Review of Books*, June 24, 1982.
1983.   'Review of *The Economics of Feasible Socialism*, by Alec Nove.'
          Dissent, Fall 1983.
1985.   'Review of *The Second Industrial Divide*, by Michael Piore and
          Charles Sabel.' *The New York Times Book Review*, January 6, 1985.
1986.   'Review of *Economics: An Alternative Text*, by Guy Routh.' *Journal
          of Economic Literature*, American Economic Association, March
          1986.
1986.   'Review of *The Rhetoric of Economics*, by Donald N. McCloskey.'
          The New York Review of Books, April 24, 1986.
1986.   'Review of *John Maynard Keynes*, Vol. 1, by Robert Skidelsky.' *The
          New York Times Book Review*, May 11, 1986.
1986.   'Review of *At the Dawn of Tyranny*, by Eli Sagan.' *Monthly Review*,
          September 1986.
1987.   'Review of *Economics in Perspective*, by John Kenneth Galbraith.'
          The New York Review of Books, November 5, 1987.
1988.   'Review of *The New Palgrave: A Dictionary of Economics*, edited by
          John Eatwell, Peter Newman and Murray Milgate.' *The New York
          Review of Books*, March 3, 1988.
1989.   'Review of *The Fatal Conceit*, by Friedrich Hayek,' *The Nation*,
          April 1989.
1989.   'Review of *Governing a $5 Trillion Dollar Economy*, by Herbert
          Stein.' *Challenge*, Aug/Sept 1989.
1989.   'Review of *Socialism, Past and Future*, by Michael Harrington.'
          Dissent, Fall 1989.

1989.   'Review of *The Privatization Decision,* by John Donahue.' *The New York Times Book Review,* December 17, 1989.

1990.   'Review of *Scale and Scope: The Dynamics of Industrial Capitalism,* by Alfred Chandler.' *The New York Review of Books,* October 11, 1990.

1991.   'Review of *The End of Laissez-Faire: National Purpose and the Global Economy After the Cold War,* by Robert Kuttner.' *Dissent,* Summer 1991.

Bibliography

Appleby, Joyce Oldham. 1978. *Economic Thought and Ideology in Seventeenth-Century England*. Princeton NJ: Princeton University Press.

Ayres, C. E. 1944 [1962]. *The Theory of Economic Progress: A Study of the Fundamentals of Economic Development and Cultural Change*, 2nd edn. New York: Schocken Books.

Blaug, Mark. 1980 [1992]. *The Methodology of Economics: Or How Economists Explain*. Cambridge: Cambridge University Press.

——. 1985. *Great Economists Since Keynes: An Introduction to the Lives & Works of One Hundred Modern Economists*. Cambridge: Cambridge University Press.

——. 1992. *The Methodology of Economics: Or How Economists Explain*. 2nd edn. Cambridge: Cambridge University Press.

Campbell, Colin. 1975. 'Economic Historian Robert Heilbroner Tells Why the World He Enjoys is Finished.' *Psychology Today*. February 1975.

Canterbery, E. Ray. 1987. *The Making of Economics*. Belmont Calif.: Wadsworth Publishing Company.

——. 1995. *The Literate Economist: A Brief History of Economics*. New York: Harper Collins College Publishers.

Galbraith, John Kenneth. 1967. *The New Industrial State*, 4th edn. New York: New American Library.

Gardner, Helen, Horst de la Croix and Richard G. Tansey. 1975 *Art Through the Ages*. 6th edn. New York: Harcourt Brace Jovanovich.

Gay, Peter. 1985. *Freud for Historians*. Oxford: Oxford University Press.

Giddens, Anthony. 1984. 'Hermeneutics and Social Theory', in Gary Shapiro and Alan Sica (eds), *Hermeneutics: Questions and Prospects*. Amherst Mass.: The University of Massachusetts Press.

Hamilton, Walton H. 1919. 'The Institutional Approach to Economic Theory', *American Economic Review*. March 1919.

Heilbroner, Robert L. 1942. 'Saving and Investment: Dynamic Aspects', *American Economic Review*. December 1942.

——. 1950. 'The American Poor', *Harper's Magazine*. June 1950.

——. [1953] 1986. *The Worldly Philosophers: The Lives, Times and Ideas of The Great Economic Thinkers*. 6th edn. New York: Simon & Schuster.

——. 1956. *The Quest For Wealth*. New York: Simon & Schuster.

——. [1959] 1960. *The Future as History: The Historic Currents of Our Time and the Direction in Which They are Taking America*. New York: Harper & Row.

——. 1962 [1993] *The Making of Economic Society*. 9th edn. Englewood Cliffs, NJ: Prentice-Hall.

——. 1963a. *The Great Ascent: The Struggle for Economic Development in Our Time*. New York: Harper & Row.

——. 1963b. *The World of Economics*. American Library Association.

——. 1965. *The Limits of American Capitalism*. New York: W. W. Norton.

——. 1966. 'Is Economic Theory Possible?' *Social Research*. Summer.

——. 1968. 'Putting Marx to Work', *The New York Review of Books*. December 5, 1968.

——. 1970a. *Between Capitalism and Socialism: Essays in Political Economics*. New York: Vintage.

——. 1970b. 'On the Limited Relevance of Economics', *Public Interest*. Fall.

——. 1970c. 'On the Possibility of a Political Economics', *Journal of Economic Issues*. December.

——. 1972. 'Interview', *Business Week*. September 30, 1972.

——. 1973. 'Economics as a "Value Free" Science', *Social Research*. Spring.

——. [1974a] 1991. *An Inquiry Into the Human Prospect: Looked at Again for the 1990s*. New York: W. W. Norton.

——. 1974b. 'The Clouded Crystal Ball', *American Economic Review*. May 1974

——. 1975. 'Marxism, Psychoanalysis and the Problem of Unified Theory of Behavior', *Social Research*. Autumn.

——. 1980. *Marxism: For and Against*. New York: W. W. Norton.

——. 1984. 'Capitalism as Gestalt: A Contrast of Visions', in *Free Market Conservatism*, Edward Nell (ed.), London: George Allen & Unwin.

——. 1985a. *The Nature and Logic of Capitalism*. New York: W. W. Norton.

——. 1985b. 'The State and Capitalism: How They Interact and Move Apart', *Dissent*. Fall.

——. 1986. *The Essential Adam Smith*. New York: W. W. Norton.

——. 1987. 'Fundamental Economic Concepts – Another Perspective', *Journal of Economic Education*. Spring.

——. 1988a. *Behind the Veil of Economics: Essays in the Worldly Philosophy*. New York: W. W. Norton.

——. 1988b. 'Capitalism', in *The New Palgrave*, John Eatwell, Murray Milgate and Peter Newman, (eds), New York and London: Macmillan.

——. 1988c. 'Wealth', in *The New Palgrave*, John Eatwell, Murray Milgate and Peter Newman (eds), New York and London: Macmillan.

——. 1988d. 'The Coming Meltdown of Traditional Capitalism', *Ethics and International Affairs*. Vol. 2.

——. 1989. 'The Triumph of Capitalism" *The New Yorker*. January 23, 1989.

——. 1990. Foreword to *Rethinking The Future: The Correspondence Between Geoffrey Vickers and Adolph Lowe*, edited by Jeanne Vickers. New Brunswick NJ: Transaction Publishers.

——. 1992a. 'Robert L. Heilbroner', in Philip Arestis and Malcolm Sawyer (eds), *A Biographical Dictionary of Dissenting Economists*. Aldershot: Edward Elgar.

——. 1992b. 'Is a Worldly Philosophy Still Possible? Adolph Lowe as Analyst and Visionary', *Review of Social Economy*. Winter 1992.

——. 1993a. *21st Century Capitalism*. New York: W. W. Norton.

——. 1993b. 'Anti-Depression Economics' *Atlantic Monthly*. April, 1993.

——. 1994. 'Vision in Economic Thought', *Journal of Economic Issues*, June 1994.

——. 1995. *Visions of the Future: The Distant Past, Yesterday, Today, Tomorrow*. New York: Oxford University Press.

——. 1996. *Teachings From The Worldly Philosophy*. New York: W. W. Norton.

Heilbroner, Robert L. and Peter L. Bernstein. 1963. *A Primer on Government Spending*. New York: Random House.
——. 1989. *The Debt and Deficit: False Alarms, Real Possibilities*. New York: W. W. Norton.
Heilbroner, Robert L. and William Milberg. 1996. *The Crisis of Vision in Modern Economic Thought*. Cambridge: Cambridge University Press.
Hirsch, E. D. Jr. 1988. *Cultural Literacy: What Every American Needs to Know*. New York: Vantage Books.
Keynes, John Maynard. 1936. *The General Theory of Employment, Interest and Money*. New York: Harcourt, Brace & World.
——. 1951. *Essays in Biography*. London: Rupert Hart-Davis.
Lange, Oscar and Fred Taylor. 1938. *On the Economic Theory of Socialism*. New York: McGraw-Hill.
Lowe, Adolph. 1935. *Economics and Sociology: A Plea for Co-operation in the Social Sciences*. London: George Allen & Unwin.
——. 1965 [1977]. *On Economic Knowledge: Toward a Science of Political Economics*. White Plains New York: M. E. Sharpe.
——. 1969. 'Toward A Science of Political Economics', in Robert L. Heilbroner (ed.), *Economic Means and Social Ends*. Englewood Cliffs, NJ: Prentice-Hall.
Mirowski, Philip. 1989. *More Heat Than Light*. New York: Cambridge University Press.
Nell Edward. 1988. *Prosperity and Public Spending: Transformational Growth and The Role of Government*. Boston: Unwin Hyman.
——. 1993a. 'Transformational Growth and Learning: Developing Craft Technology Into Scientific Mass Production', in R. Thompson (ed.), *Learning and Technological Change*. New York: St Martin's Press.
——. 1993b. 'Introduction: History and Vision in Economics', in *Economics as Worldly Philosophy: Essays in Honor of Robert L. Heilbroner*, edited by Ron Blackwell, Jaspal Chatha and Edward J. Nell. New York: St Martin's Press.
Nell, Edward J. and Thomas F. Phillips. 1995. 'Transformational Growth and The Business Cycle.' *Eastern Economic Journal*. Vol. 21, No. 2. Spring 1995.
Okroi, Loren J. 1988. *Galbraith, Harrington, Heilbroner: Economists and Dissent in an Age of Optimism*. Princeton NJ: Princeton University Press.
Polanyi, Karl 1944. *The Great Transformation: The Political and Economic Origins of Our Time*. Boston: Beacon Press.
——. 1968. 'Aristotle Discovers the Economy', in Geo. Dalton (ed.), *Primitive, Archaic, and Modern Economies: Essays by Karl Polanyi*. Garden City New York: Doubleday.
Robbins, Lionel. [1932] 1949. *An Essay on the Nature and Significance of Economic Science*. 2nd edn. London: Macmillan.
Sahlins, Marshall. 1972. *Stone Age Economics*. Aldine, New York: Hawthorne.
Schumpeter, Joseph. 1942. *Capitalism, Socialism and Democracy*. New York: Harper & Row.
——. 1954. *History of Economic Analysis*. Oxford: Oxford University Press.
——. 1979. *Theory of Economic Development*. Cambridge Mass.: Harvard University Press.

Shapiro, Gary and Alan Sica. 1984. 'Introduction', in Gary Shapiro and Alan Sica (eds), *Hermeneutics: Questions and Prospects*. Amherst Mass.: The University of Massachusetts Press.

Sheinbaum, Stanley and Nathan Gardels. 1989. 'The Triumph of Capitalism', *New Perspective Quarterly*. Fall 1989.

Smith, Adam. 1776. *An Inquiry Into The Causes and Wealth of Nations*. New York: Random House.

Stanfield, J. Ron. 1995. 'Phenomena and epiphenomenon in Economics', *Economics, Power and Culture: Essays in the Development of Radical Institutionalism*. London: Macmillan Press.

Thurow, Lester. 1996. *The Future of Capitalism: How Today's Economic Forces Shape Tomorrow's World*. New York: Morrow.

Van Dyne, Larry. 1978. 'Robert Heilbroner on the Doom of Capitalism', *The Chronicle Review*. October 16, 1978.

Veblen, Thorstein. 1898. 'Why Economics is not a Science,' *The Quarterly Journal of Economics*. Vol. xii, July 1898.

Vickers, Jeanne. 1990. *Rethinking The Future: The Correspondence Between Geoffrey Vickers and Adolph Lowe*. New Brunswick NJ: Transaction Publishers.

Wachterhauser, Brice R. 1986. 'Introduction: History and Language in Understanding', in Brice Wachterhauser (ed.), *Hermeneutics and Modern Philosophy*. Albany New York: State University of New York Press.

Index

115

This book provides an intellectual portrait of Robert Heilbroner. It traces the development of his work and places it within the literature of economic thought. This work shows that Heilbroner is a writer of political economy in the classical sense. His work is more reminiscent of Adam Smith or Karl Marx than of contemporary economic theorists. Heilbroner's economics is built on a solid foundation of social psychology, evolutionary dynamics and human history.

This book begins with a brief look at Heilbroner's life and influences. It traces his academic career and highlights his major publications. Next, it turns to Heilbroner's criticisms of traditional economic theory. It finds that Heilbroner believes traditional economics acts as a 'veil' which obscures the true workings of the capitalist order. It then moves to an examination of his 'hermeneutic' methodology and his explanation of the structure of capitalism. It shows that capitalism is best viewed as a regime with a clear history and future tendency. The study then carefully examines his views on the future of capitalism. It concludes with a final appraisal of his political economy and places him within the history of economic thought.

Michael C. Carroll is Assistant Professor of Economics at Muskingum College. He is active in the fields on social economics, institutional thought and regional development. Apart from his academic experience, Professor Carroll's research draws on his extensive private sector background. He is former operations manager of manufacturing firms and a former controller for a group of steel companies.